Mary McLeod Bethune

Mary

also by Catherine Owens Peare, "Mahatma Gandhi," etc.

Catherine Owens Peare

McLeod Bethune

The Vanguard Press, Inc.   *New York*

Ninth Printing

Copyright, 1951, by Catherine Owens Peare

*Published simultaneously in Canada by the
Copp Clark Company, Ltd., Toronto*

*Designed by Jerome Kuhl
Manufactured in the United States of America
by H. Wolff, New York, N.Y.*

A Foreword to My Young Readers

All my life I have worked with youth. I have begged for them and fought for them and lived for them and in them. My story is their story.

Because I see young Mary McLeod in all struggling boys and girls, I can never rest while there is still something that I can do to make the ground firmer under their feet, to make their efforts more productive, to bring their goals nearer, to make their faith in God and their fellow men a little stronger. May those who read this volume, into which Catherine Owens Peare has put such unstinted labor and so much understanding, gather from it new confidence in themselves, new faith in God, and a willingness to work hard to reach the goals of a good life.

Mine has not been an easy road. Very few of my generation

found life easy or wanted it that way. Your road may be somewhat less rugged because of the struggles we have made. The doors of progress and advancement will open to the steady, persistent pressure of your skilled hands and your trained minds, your stout hearts and your prayers, more readily than they opened to me.

I rejoice now, as I look back down my seventy-five years, that I have been able to share in our great American life. I rejoice that I have been able to help in the movement for the extension of brotherhood through greater interracial understanding. I rejoice that in my own way I have been able to demonstrate that there is a place in God's sun for the youth "farthest down" who has the vision, the determination, and the courage to reach it.

Mary McLeod Bethune

Daytona Beach, 1950.

*All poems used as chapter
subtitles have been written by
American Negro poets.*

Contents

Illustrations

Acknowledgments

The author wishes to express sincere thanks to the following for their generous help:

Mrs. Bessie F. Bailey, secretary to Mrs. Bethune at Bethune-Cookman College

Miss Julia Baxter, research specialist of the National Association for the Advancement of Colored People

Mrs. Ruth Brall, sculptor

Mrs. Harold T. Butts, Ormond Beach, Florida

Miss Margie L. Carter, County Supervisor of Schools, Lee County, South Carolina

Mrs. Charlotte Ford Clark, Dean of Instruction, Bethune-Cookman College

Mr. and Mrs. A. T. Cordery, Barber-Scotia College

President L. S. Cozart, Barber-Scotia College

Mr. Julius Davidson, publisher of *The News-Journal*, Daytona Beach, Florida

Mrs. Arabella Denniston, secretary to Mrs. Bethune in Washington, D.C.

Dr. Dorothy Boulding Ferebee, President of the National Council of Negro Women, Inc.

Mr. Charles Francis, head dietician, Bethune-Cookman College

Mrs. Mame Mason Higgins, Counselor of Women, Bethune-Cookman College

Mr. Eugene K. Jones, formerly General Secretary of the National Urban League

Dr. Rayford W. Logan, Director of The Association for the Study of Negro Life and History, Inc.

Mr. Harold V. Lucas, Mrs. Bethune's first trained secretary, now an instructor at Bethune-Cookman College

Miss Arenia C. Mallory, Principal of Saints Industrial School, Lexington, Mississippi

Mrs. Mary E. Mason, Daytona Beach, Florida

Mrs. Bertha Loving Mitchell, Secretary-Treasurer, Bethune-Volusia Beach, Inc.

Mr. Benjamin Mitchell, Director of the Pinehaven Project in Daytona Beach, Florida

Dr. Richard V. Moore, President of Bethune-Cookman College

Mr. Guichard Parris, Director of Promotion and Publicity of the National Urban League

Mr. Asa Philip Randolph, International President of the Brotherhood of Sleeping Car Porters

Mrs. Eleanor Roosevelt

Mrs. Cecelia Cantey Smith, Washington, D.C.

Mrs. Frances Procter Taylor, Bethune-Cookman College

Mrs. Mary Church Terrell, Washington, D.C.

Dr. Channing H. Tobias, Director of the Phelps-Stokes Fund

Mrs. Chauncey L. Waddell, Member of the Board of Directors

of the United Negro College Fund, Inc., and Associate
Chairman of its National Council

Mr. Walter White, Executive Secretary of the National Association for the Advancement of Colored People

Mrs. Ruth Danenhower Wilson, author of *Jim Crow Joins Up*

Dr. Ralph J. Young, Baltimore, Maryland

Mary McLeod Bethune

Alas! and am I born for this,
To wear this slavish chain?

"On Liberty and Slavery" by George Moses Horton

I. *Days of Ceaseless Toil*

Mary Jane turned in her sleep and turned again, cautious of the spears that poked through the mattress and pricked her skin. A coarse sacking, stuffed with straw, that rustled and crackled when she moved about, was all the bed she had, for she was a Negro child. Feather tickings and linen covers were for white folk.

She woke up, because she knew from habit that it was morning, even though a peek through a knothole in the pine-board wall told her it was still pitch-dark outside, and she lay waiting for one of her sisters or brothers to jostle her arm and say:

"Get up, child! It's morning."

Five o'clock was rising time the year round, for on a cotton farm the work was never done, and not a minute of the day could be wasted. Mary jumped out of bed, exchanged her nightshirt for a cotton dress, and ran to the kitchen, the room that everybody loved. There she found her mother where she knew she would find her: standing at the big iron stove, fixing breakfast of bacon fat back, hominy grits, and coffee. The room was steamy warm from the cooking—too warm; even in January South Carolina isn't very cold. An oil lamp on the table flickered feebly.

"Go wash, child," her mother reminded her.

"Can we eat soon?"

"Soon as your chores are done. Now, go wash."

Mary ran out of the kitchen door to the back porch, tossing the pigtails into which her kinky hair was plaited.

A big wooden tub of water stood on the back porch, and her brothers and sisters were washing in it. There were seventeen McLeod children, fourteen of them older than Mary, some married and living in cabins of their own by now. Sally, the oldest, had gone all the way to a city to live; coming home only once for a visit, dressed in beautiful clothes and bringing a trunkful of presents with her. A host of McLeods still gathered about the tub every morning to wash, so that Mary had to wait her turn.

"Hurry up!"

"Hush up!"

"Stop quarreling and get to your chores."

Beds must be made before breakfast, the mule must be hitched to the plow, and the cow led to pasture. Mary was only nine; so to her fell the simple responsibility of leading the cow out to the field. She plunged her hands into the cold water, already grayed with other washings, tried to rub up a lather from the crude soap made by her mother from caustic soda and rendered fat, and sluiced her face with the results. A quick wash-up quickly finished, and she was off to the cowshed.

"C'mon," she ordered the cow as she took hold of the lead. "C'mon, I gotta eat breakfast."

The animal followed meekly as Mary's bare black feet found their familiar way along the path to the pasture. A thin sliver of pinkish light was just beginning to show along the horizon. When it was light enough to see, it would be light enough to work. The land all around the McLeod farm began to be visible: furrowed acres where the cotton would be planted, and beyond that flat and swampy wasteland, dismal country to anyone who didn't love it and who didn't call it home.

Bouncing back in through the kitchen door, Mary found the older members of the family already eating breakfast. Again the youngest had to wait, because the table wasn't big enough to accommodate everyone at one sitting.

When the last dish was washed and the last pot scoured and hung away, the whole family—Samuel and Patsy McLeod and the seven or eight of their seventeen children who still lived home, the youngest a nursing infant—left their four-room cabin and started for the cotton fields.

This was plowing time; the new cotton season was starting.

They walked cautiously on their bare feet, avoiding the rows of sharp stubble left from last year's cotton crop. The family mule, called Old Bush because of his bushy tail, was standing hitched to a wide-bladed plow, and he tossed his head when the family approached him. Slowly he pulled the plow along the same furrows he had pulled it along last year, piling mounds of earth on each side, a McLeod at his head to guide him, another at the plow. The mule was the most valuable asset that the family had.

The McLeods broke their backs over the land, but they worked with love, because the land was their own. They were free. Patsy and Samuel had been slaves, made to work from sunup to sunset on someone else's land, with no profit to themselves. Then came the Civil War and Abraham Lincoln's Emancipation Proclamation that had set them free. Their older children had been slaves, too; Mary Jane and the two younger than she had been born in freedom.

Patsy McLeod left the field during the morning and sat down under a shade tree to nurse her youngest, Hattie. Toward the middle of the day she went back to the cabin to prepare the midday meal.

Mary watched her mother leave the field. Soon they could flop down on the ground near the cabin and nap. Soon there would be hot rice and black-eyed peas mixed with ham, steaming in bowls and waiting for them.

"I'm tired."

"Tend your work. We're all tired."

The plowed rows had to be spread with fertilizer, then worked again with a finer plow. Soon the rows would be smoothed off with a harrow and the earth would be ready for the precious cotton seed. A few more days and they'd be able to plant their crop, each acre taking a bushel of seed. The earth needed as much care and tending as the nursing infant.

A call from the cabin told them that the midday meal was ready, and the little group of all ages and sizes straggled in from the field. Samuel McLeod was a tall, muscular man, a head or more above any of his brood. He looked at them lovingly as they walked between the furrows, then looked back at the small figure lagging behind the others.

"C'mon, Mary Jane. What you lagging behind for?"

"I'm dreaming."

"What about?"

"About God, mostly."

"That's proper dreaming, but ain't you hungry?"

Yes, she was famished! Brought out of her reverie by the suggestion, Mary bolted ahead and reached the door before the others.

Her father laughed at her fondly. That little one! Always different from the others!

Again there was the jostling and pushing around the big wooden tub so that all hands could be washed before eating. Again the smallest were pushed aside by the older ones. Again the two sittings at the table.

Back to the field the McLeod family trudged, to labor until dark. The seasons did not wait.

At last, against the dim light of the setting sun, the silhouettes of the weary McLeods moved slowly home to rest.

They were quieter around the supper table, and after supper there were still more household chores before evening prayers. Mary tended to the lamps, carrying each from its place to the kitchen table, washing and polishing its glass chimney, trimming its wick, adding to the kerosene in the brass bowl, then carrying it back.

Before the living-room fireplace that Samuel McLeod had fashioned of clay long ago, close to the warmth of the fire, rocking gently, sat the one McLeod who hadn't gone to the fields to labor: Grandmother Sophia. She had spent her whole life in slavery; now she could sit at ease, a red bandanna tied around her wiry gray wool, sucking on a long-stemmed pipe stuck between her toothless gums. Grandmother Sophia chatted constantly in a low voice, to her family when they were about, to God when they were not.

"Dear God, I am so happy to be living in this loving family, where I can get hot biscuits and butter, and coffee with cream, sitting at my own fireplace."

Mary finished her lamps and ran to her grandmother. This was the part of the evening she liked best, because they would sing hymns. She dragged a small brown footstool over in front of the wood box near grandmother, so that she could sit close to the old lady's feet and lean back against the box. Grandmother knew things that others did not.

"We used to belong to the Wilson plantation," Grandmother explained. "We used to belong to the Wilsons and the McLeods."

"Can they take us back?" Mary always asked.

"No, child, no!" her grandmother always assured her. "We're free."

Mary Jane usually goaded her grandmother with questions, so that she would tell at least one of her stories. Mary liked best the story of Queen Esther pleading with the king for her people.

Patsy McLeod came to the fireplace and sank down into a rocker. Samuel came, too, and eased his tall figure into an overstuffed green Morris chair, being careful of its broken springs. The rest of the children gathered about, and Samuel McLeod began the first hymn:

"Free at last,
Free at last,
I thank God I'm free at last.

"Way down yonder in the graveyard walk,
I thank God I'm free at last,
Me and my Jesus gwineter meet and talk,
I thank God I'm free at last. . . ."

Heads bowed reverently in prayer after the singing. Each prayed silently, and whoever cared to pray aloud did so. No hymnbook was held and no Bible read, because none of them could read or write.

Mary closed her eyes and swayed back and forth on her footstool to the rhythm of the singing. She held tight to her grandmother's hand while they prayed, feeling herself lifted, lifted. God always came to her, she knew, and she loved those family prayers.

Soon it was time for bed again, and Mary fell down on her straw mattress, in slumberland almost immediately. Praying always made her sleep well.

The seasons moved on, and workday followed workday. After plowing was finished, the fields had to be planted, and the McLeods waited for those first tiny green spears to show above the ground, each cotton plant putting up two leaves. There would be too many plants, and the McLeods had to go out into the field and "chop out" the extra plants with their hoes.

Then came the battle with the crab grass. Crab grass grew everywhere. It kept popping out of the ground, trying to kill the delicate cotton plants. Too much rain during April meant that the crab grass would grow even faster.

Chop, chop, chop with the hoe. Mary had to take her place with the others to keep the fields clean of grass and weeds. Only the infant and Grandmother Sophia were exempted from the long, long days in the boiling hot sun, forever chopping, chopping at the crab grass.

"Oh, Lord, deliver me," Mary would pray as she bent to her labor.

When she saw her mother pause, lean on her hoe, and gaze at the position of the sun, shading her eyes with her hand, Mary knew it would soon be time for the midday meal.

The cotton grew slowly for the next three months. Cotton had to be cultivated by hand; too much machinery would make it wither and die. The plants pushed their way upward until they were tall as shrubs, up to the waists of the adults but towering over Mary's head. She felt as though she were in a dense forest, where all the trees were alike. Still she must chop, chop, chop at the crab grass; as she traveled down each row she watched the tips of the delicate branches for the first sign of a bud, three leaves folded intricately together to form a square, inside of that square the beginnings of a blossom.

Chop, chop . . . The sun grew hotter in the sky and burned deeper into their skin, but they could not leave their cotton fields. A rainy day was a welcome relief from the South Carolina heat, though as soon as the rain passed the crab grass would begin inching up around the precious plants.

Chop, chop . . . Suddenly there was a shout.

"Snake! Snake!"

All the McLeod children dropped their hoes, racing toward the sound, the taller ones leaping over the rows, and the hunt was on. The harmless garter snake slithered over the ground, trying to escape, but he was marked for destruction as Mary and her brothers and sisters raced after him, surrounded him, shouted and pushed with excitement, and trampled him to death.

Patsy and Samuel only smiled at each other, because they had seen this same episode many times before. They knew the children were stealing time out for a little play, and they didn't scold, because they realized that children have to play once in a while.

When the snake had been destroyed, and destroyed again, so that he couldn't possibly need any more attention, the young McLeods walked slowly back to their battle with the weeds.

"Dear Lord," Mary muttered as she picked up her hoe. "Why does cotton take so long to grow?"

She watched where she chopped, lest she harm a plant, and she watched the branches. She wanted to be the first to spy a bud; so did her brothers and sisters. There was definite glory and distinction in finding the first bud.

"Let me be the first," she prayed.

As if in direct answer to her petition, there it was! Just at a level with her eyes, that tiny green square! She stopped and looked closer to make certain of her discovery. Then she burst into a shout:

"Here it is! Here it is!"

All the McLeods left their work on this cry and raced to Mary's side. There it was! The cotton was budding. Now they could measure their time. Now they knew just how much longer it would be before they could take their crop to market. In exactly three weeks the flaming red blossoms would turn the field to scarlet. On the third day of its life each blossom would wither and drop its petals, and in their place would be a pod. In six more weeks the pod would ripen into a full-grown cotton boll, a creamy white fluff, bursting out of its five-pointed green star, and the whole field and the fields of all their neighbors would be white, glaring white in the midday sun, ghostly white by moonlight.

It happened this way every year, yet every year it was just as exciting. The McLeods loved their cotton as much as they loved one another.

They were still excited when they walked in from the field for the last meal of the day. During evening prayers they prayed for the cotton, and after prayers they sat outside and chatted about their cotton.

Mary raced about collecting the lamps, trimming their wicks and polishing their chimneys, so that she could join her family. On this hot, still July night, she knew what they would want her to do: fix smoke sticks to keep the mosquitoes away. She gathered some pieces of kindling, wrapped old rags around the tips, dipped them in crude oil, and held a match to them. The crude oil caught fire and gave out a suffocating black smoke.

"Here," she said, running out and giving the smoking sticks to one and another. "This'll keep the skeeters away."

Far down the road other Negro families were sitting outside of their own rude cabins, and the glowing tips of their smoke sticks could be seen waving about in the dark.

Mary perched on the doorsill. Maybe they would forget for a few minutes that her bedtime had come and gone.

July nights were the dreamingest. She could hug her knees and stare at the stars in the sky. If she stared hard at one of them, it would split in two. Or she could stare out at the shadowy fields where she knew there were rows and rows of budding cotton. No matter how you stared at cotton, you couldn't see it grow. No matter how you listened, you could never hear it. You could hear corn grow on a hot, breathless night. It rustled and whispered. But not cotton. Cotton was as proud and shy as a white lady in a big house.

"Bedtime, children," came the order shattering her reverie, and the youngest had to troop off to their straw mattresses.

Mother came into the house, too, because she had ironing to do before she could go to bed. Even after working in the fields all day, she managed to wash and iron clothes for the white folk and bring a few extra pennies into the household.

As Mary closed her eyes she knew that tomorrow morning her mother would have to deliver the wash before she went into the field. She hoped Mama would let her go, too.

That was just how it happened.

Directly after breakfast her mother picked up the big bundle of wash, balanced it on her head, and started along the winding dirt road across the branch, with Mary tagging along.

Mary was happy, so happy that she burst into song:

"Oh, I'm a gwineter sing, gwineter sing,
  Gwineter sing all along the way.
Oh, I'm a-gwineter sing, gwineter sing,
  Gwineter sing all along the way."

Suddenly she stopped and listened. Several seconds of close examination revealed in the tall grass an early-morning competitor. The slim green body of a katydid sat completely protected by the matching color of the leaf.

"You're happy, too! Don't stop singing."

"Come on, Mary," called her mother, turning her head slowly, balancing the bundle with one hand.

On they went down the road, until one more curve brought the white outline of their destination into view. There was the big house, many times larger than the McLeod cabin and with not nearly so many people in it. They turned in at the gravel driveway that swept past the gigantic white pillars.

The front entrance was not for them, so they stepped off the drive to a footpath along the side of the house to the rear entrance and knocked at the door. This was the home of Patsy McLeod's former owner, Ben Wilson.

The door opened to admit Patsy, and Mary waited outside. A bluebottle zoomed up from nowhere to plague her ears, and she tossed her head about and waved her hands around her head to get rid of him.

She walked along the path with the hope of discouraging the buzzing fly, and a few yards from the house she saw what she knew was the playhouse. White children had to have a special house of their own, just to play in.

Mary peeked in through the open door and saw two golden-haired girls about her own age, Ben Wilson's grandchildren.

"Hello, Mary," said one. "Do you want to come in?"

Mary inched her way in and gazed about in wonderment at the dolls, the toys, the diminutive furniture, the dishes, the clothes. How white folk did dress up! Even the dolls had on silk dresses—and shoes!

"Would you like to hold one of my dolls?"

The shoeless guest eased herself into one of the scaled-down chairs while a magnificent doll was laid in her lap.

"Yes, Ma'am!"

"And look, Mary! Here is a new dress for my doll that Mother just gave me. Isn't it pretty?"

"It sure is!"

"Let's play we're keeping house. You mind my baby for me, while I have tea."

Mary waited for further instructions.

"Mary, can't you make the baby stop crying?" said the little hostess in imitation of her elders. "He's spoiling my tea."

With the natural mothering tenderness of her kind, Mary held the make-believe baby close to lull its crying. She got up and walked about with the doll, patting its bottom, improvising a lullaby. En route around the room she paused as her attention was attracted to an object on a little stand: a book. She reached out and picked it up.

The golden curls flounced themselves across the room, and a quick hand snatched the book away.

"Put down that book! *You* can't read!"

The words stabbed deeply.

"I wasn't going to hurt it," protested the startled, angry black child.

"How do I know that? Anyway, books are for people who can read."

"Can you read what it says, Miss?"

'Of course I can. Now give me back my doll, too."

Mary surrendered the silken-clad toy and ran out of the playhouse, out of the inhospitable atmosphere, out into the clean morning sunlight. What had she done? Touched something she shouldn't, and her whole happy morning was spoiled.

"Come along, Mary," she heard her mother call from the

door of the big house, and she fled toward the sound that suddenly gave direction to her confusion. Ahead of her mother, she pad-padded down the gravel drive to the road as they started back to the cabin.

What was the trouble between black folk and white, she pondered as she walked along. She had just touched something, just touched something, that was all.

How come white folk had such big houses and fine clothes? They had glass in their windows that had to be polished until it shone and glistened in the sun. They had colored folk in the house to do all the work, and carriages to ride in whenever they went out.

"Dear Lord," she prayed. "I don't think we're so free."

As the Negro cabins came into sight she saw them in their true perspective for the first time. What had been happy homes an hour before were shabby, unpainted pine-board shacks. A few had sagging porches at the front, and the pillars holding up the roofs that extended over the porches looked like kindling strips compared with the massive columns of the great house she had just visited. The McLeod cabin leaned a little to one side, as though the ground had sunk away from it.

How come? How come? How come white folk had so much and colored folk so little? Maybe the difference between them was just this matter of reading and writing.

"I'm going to learn to read!" she resolved, kicking up the road dust with her toes. "I'm going to learn to read!"

I know why the caged bird beats his wing
Till its blood is red on the cruel bars.

"Sympathy" by Paul Laurence Dunbar

2. *The Cry of the Soul To Know*

When they reached their own land they walked straight out into the field and joined the rest of the family, bending over their hoes or cultivating the rows of earth between the cotton plants. Mary Jane picked up a hoe and began her daily pursuit of the crab grass. The cotton was growing fast. After the first bud, others seemed to pop out all over.

"Please, God," she said aloud as she worked. "Please, God, let me learn to read—somehow."

The August sun grew hotter, and the air was still. Beads of moisture stood out on her forehead, and her cotton dress stuck to her sweaty body. Chop, chop . . .

When she was out of sight of the rest of the family, she

laid down her hoe and sank to her knees in the soft, red-brown earth. Lifting her hands and face to the sky, she prayed:

"Please, dear Lord, let me learn. Deliver me from the crab grass. Please, God, I want to go to school."

Footsteps interrupted her, and she jumped up. Lunch time! The family was leaving the field, and Mary Jane ran to catch up with her father.

"Can I ever go to school?" she asked Samuel, trotting to keep up with his long-legged stride.

"There isn't any school," he told her.

"If I could read, I could read the Bible."

Samuel didn't answer. There were many things that he and Patsy could not explain to their children. They could only let them discover for themselves the difficulties of being a Negro. When Mary Jane or the other children came to them with bewildering questions: "Why can't I do this?" or "Why can't I do that?" or "Why must I always go around to the back door?" Patsy and Samuel could only shake their heads sadly and reply, "Child, you're colored."

Samuel McLeod took hold of Mary Jane's hand, and they walked along together. Of all his children, Mary Jane was the strangest and best. She prayed harder, worked faster, dreamed more. She was like her mother, intelligent, quick, determined, full of spirit.

Patsy was the descendant of a royal African prince. She walked with a queenly bearing, spoke in a gentle voice, and ran her household with firm efficiency, giving the plodding, easygoing Samuel the steering and guidance that he needed.

"I don't know where Mama got her high ideals of morals and cleanliness," Mary McLeod Bethune once said of her mother. "And her efficiency in everything she did. She had no books, no learning, but she was wonderfully undergirded spiritually."

When Patsy and Samuel had married, they were slaves working on different plantations, and they had had to wait a long time for permission to wed. Slaves were not generally allowed weddings; many were not allowed to choose their mates. Often, a wife or husband would be sold to another plantation, separating the couple and breaking up what wretched little home life they had. Children were certain to be snatched from them as soon as they were old enough to work. Slaves were not people; they were property, with a high market value.

Samuel told his master that he wanted to marry a slave who belonged to a nearby plantation.

"You will have to buy her yourself, Sam," he was told.

"Thank you, Massah."

Sam worked hard on that promise. His opportunities to earn money were few and limited, but he managed. When his tasks on the McLeod plantation allowed him free time, he would hire himself out to other white men for field labor, cotton picking, corn husking. Humble, easygoing Sam at last accumulated the price of his bride, and he took the money to his owner.

"Will you buy her for me now, Massah McLeod? Will you go get Pat for me?"

"Yes, Sam; I'll go get her for you."

Patsy had been waiting for the day, too. Smiling and shy, she was brought to the McLeod plantation, where she caught her first glimpse of Sam, standing by the roadside and watching eagerly for the low-sided wagon to draw up. He rushed forward to help her down from her crouching position in the back while his master jumped down from the seat in front.

"Here she is, Sam."

"Yes, Sir, Massah! Thank you, Sir."

Not all slaves were as lucky as they! Not all slaves would

have been allowed such happiness, let alone a real wedding. On that happy day long tables of food were spread under the trees, and a crowd of guests, both Negro and white, gathered to see Sam, in a suit of his master's, wedded to Patsy, her white veil gleaming in the afternoon sun. Nearby stood the big mansion to which Sam and Patsy and whatever children they might have would belong.

As Sam walked between the rows of cotton plants, holding Mary Jane by the hand, he marveled that they did not belong to anyone, but Mary Jane didn't understand that. During slavery a child as big as she might have been taken away from its parents and sent to a distant plantation to be hand-maiden to a white man's daughter. Sam felt grateful to the white world for letting him keep his wife and children. He would not want to live if he lost any one of them.

The sultry, hot August days passed one after another, and the cotton thrived, putting forth its magnificent blossoms all over Lee and Sumter counties. Backs bent and hands toiled as the bolls developed, and suddenly at the end of September it was cotton-picking time.

Joy! Excitement! as the blobs of white fluff stood out on the brittle black branches and the Negroes went down the rows picking at feverish speed.

Mary Jane did this best. She could pick two hundred fifty pounds of cotton a day. With a burlap sack bigger than herself slung over her left shoulder, working with both hands, she could deftly snap off cotton bolls until her hands were full, then reach back and pop them into the bag.

The Negroes laughed and sang and joked as they picked the cotton. It was a good crop this year; it would bring a good price. As soon as it was sold they could pay their debts, buy supplies, and have a little money left over for fun.

Mary McLeod worked with a sober face, because her mind

had become obsessed with another fever: the desire to read.

"Dear Lord," she prayed as her skillful fingers flew from boll to boll, "help me to get educated."

It was hopeless, though; no school, no books, no teacher; only cotton, cotton, cotton, season after season. When they weren't working in the cotton, the McLeods had to tend the paddy of rice growing in the swampy ground at the edge of their property, or they had to gather fodder or weed the vegetable patch.

"I want to read! I want to read!" Mary prayed over and over as she filled her sack.

When the gunny sack would hold no more, she started toward the cabin to empty its contents on the ground; and as she bent over to roll the heavy burden from her back, she found herself standing before a stranger. Mary Jane McLeod looked up into the kindest face she had ever seen in her life, a Negro face, yet much paler than her own. Mary's skin was coal black, and the woman before her, dressed in city clothes, was a light tan.

"I'm Miss Wilson, Mary."

Miss? Negroes were never given titles; they were never *mistered* or *missed*.

The whole family had come in from the field to gather about this visitor, this Emma Wilson who had interrupted their work in the busiest season of the year.

Patsy put her arm around the one child in the family who was different—Mary Jane.

"We can spare this one," said Patsy to Miss Wilson.

The whole family nodded their heads in agreement. Yes, it must be Mary Jane who went.

"She's a homely child but she's the brightest," put in Samuel.

Miss Wilson smiled at Mary and explained: "The Mission Board of the Presbyterian Church has sent me down here to start a school for Negro children, and I want you to come to Mayesville as soon as the cotton picking is finished."

"I'm gonna read? You mean I'm gonna read, Miss Wilson?" cried Mary excitedly, her voice suddenly hoarse as the tears streamed down her face.

She had prayed, and God had answered her prayers!

"Thank you, Ma'am," she mumbled, and sinking to her knees she stretched her hands to the sky once more. "Thank you, God, for delivering me."

Pat clasped her hands before her face and said, "Thank you, Master."

Sam agreed reverently, "Yes, Pat."

Emma Wilson smiled, patted Mary on the head, and went on down the dusty road to other Negro cabins, to beg for more children for her school. She wanted them all, but she knew their families would not give them up. She would be lucky if she could glean one child from each crowded cabin.

Emma Wilson had returned to the South to liberate her people with education, the only real road to freedom, and after witnessing Mary McLeod's deep passion to learn, her own hopes ran wild. One child like Mary Jane could make all the heartbreak worth while.

The McLeods walked back to their cotton picking, and Mary galloped ahead of them, trailing an empty sack behind her.

"Come on!" she rebuked them. "Hurry up! Get that cotton picked. Don't be so slow. I gotta go to school!"

The words, "Put down that book! *You* can't read!" were going to be erased from her soul.

From shrub to shrub she traveled at a new high speed as the bolls disappeared from their stems. Two hundred fifty pounds a day? She could do better than that.

"I'm gonna read," she chanted to the rhythm of her picking. "I'm gonna get educated."

Her father grinned wide and shook his head good-naturedly. Janie was as hard-working as her mother had ever been.

Patsy had worked hard from the day Sam had married her, helping him to acquire the farm, pay off the mortgage, add more land to what they already had. The first years of their married life had been spent on the McLeod plantation, where the first fourteen of their children were born. When the slaves were emancipated, they remained on the McLeod land as sharecroppers, while Patsy went back to her former owner, Ben Wilson, to earn enough money to buy their first five acres from him. Eventually Sam and Patsy were able to increase their holdings to thirty-five acres. Samuel and his oldest sons built the cabin in which Mary was born, dragging wet clay from the nearby swamp to fashion the fireplace.

Mayesville had not been a battleground in the Civil War, and so did not have to make as drastic a recovery as some other parts of the South. General Sherman and his army had marched from Savannah, Georgia, to Columbia, South Carolina, a city forty-odd miles from Mayesville, but his wide path of burning, killing, looting, and destruction had not quite reached that little town.

During the first decade after the Civil War, Patsy and Samuel, by being cautious and wise and deferential in their dealings with white folk, had been able to develop their land unmolested. At the end of the second decade their patience and industry were being rewarded by a new hope—learning.

Mary picked cotton in a frenzy until the sun sank below the horizon, and when the family at last came in from the field and set down their sacks, she wiped the sweat from her forehead with the inside of her elbow. Her first excitement was spent, but the fires still burned white-hot within her, and at dinner table she sat dazed and silent.

Family prayers this night held special significance; she had no requests to make because they had all been granted; she had only thanks, thanks, more thanks to give. Not far from where they sat praying together was the Bible on a long table under the window. Unused because no one could read, it had lain there for years on a much-laundered shawl, with its companion pieces: a blue china pitcher, a sewing box, and an oil lamp. Soon—thank you, God—soon she would open the Book and read it to her family.

" 'Lord, I want to be a Christian in my heart,' " her mother began to sing, and Mary added her voice to the others'. Her voice was growing stronger, richer, deeper, as she matured.

Afterward the McLeods went out of doors and flung themselves on the ground in front of the cabin. The cotton that stood in mounds nearby would soon be packed into the open wagon, with boards added to the sides, and hauled to the cotton gin.

Mary felt herself under a magic spell. A miracle had just happened to her, and she strolled over to look at the cotton. With a jump and a turn she landed right in the middle of the pile and leaned back to stare at the sky.

Millions of stars tonight!

We shall not always plant while others reap
The golden increment of bursting fruit,
Not always countenance, abject and mute,
That lesser men should hold their brothers
    cheap.

"From the Dark Tower" by Countee Cullen

3. *Climbing Jacob's Ladder*

Mary stood on one bare foot and then the other, clutching her father's hand, as together they surveyed the contents of the Mayesville general store. Sam had money to spare—not much, but enough so that he could buy his daughter a gift for her first day at school.

He had hauled his cotton crop over the narrow, dusty road into town, sold it, and trudged faithfully around paying his debts: mortgage, last spring's seed and fertilizer, groceries. His hand in his pocket fingered the cash that was left. This was the one time in the year when the Negroes could indulge in little luxuries, a time of celebration. Some celebrated so childishly that their money was gone in a few hours and they had to ask for credit for next year's cotton seed and the food they would need through the winter. Sam McLeod was too industrious for that; his money must be spent carefully: a piece of dress goods for Patsy, some new candles, a few apples, a strip of bacon.

One purchase more—for Mary Jane.

"What do you want?" he asked her.

"Something to write with," she begged.

The storekeeper saw that help was needed, and he took down from the shelf a slate to which a piece of chalk was attached with a short string.

"I think this would be best," said the storekeeper. "Because, look, you can write and erase, write and erase."

Mary reached out with her square-fingered hands that were already too large from heavy work and gathered the treasure to her. She tested the chalk on the slate. Yes, it would make a mark. She could write and erase, write and erase. As soon as she learned how, she could write, write, write.

"Don't drop it; it's brittle," cautioned the man behind the counter as father and daughter left the store.

Home they lumbered in the empty wagon drawn by the mule that had as many tasks as the family members themselves.

Excitement filled the cabin and the yard when the wagon returned. Tomorrow was the day! Tomorrow was Janie's first day at school.

"You can teach us," declared her brothers and sisters.

"Oh, yes," she promised.

"Tomorrow night you can start reading to us."

"I don't know. Maybe, if I learn fast."

The ironing her mother did that night after family prayers was for Mary: a fresh new gingham dress.

She stood in their midst the next morning, like a queen among her adoring subjects, dressed and ready for the new adventure, the gingham dress starched as stiff as a board. On her feet were heavy brogans their toes covered with metal tips to lengthen their life. Her hair was combed and parted into geometric squares, each square brought together into a tight pigtail that bore a red ribbon bow on its tip. In one hand she carried a pail of luncheon, in the other hand the precious slate.

While Patsy fussed over her dress, Sam laid a loving hand on her head.

"Don't dream along the road," he cautioned her. "Don't be late the first day."

She started out of the cabin as the family stood in the door-way and watched her go. Five miles along a narrow, dusty road she must walk; five miles to the village of Mayesville and five miles back, every day.

Miss Wilson's first school was the tiny living room of a shack in the Negro quarter near the railroad track. She hoped before too much longer to have a school building of her own.

She stood in the door waiting to see how many of those children who had been promised to her would actually arrive. A handful of boys and girls put in an appearance; timid, curious, afraid of what would happen to them, they huddled together in the middle of the room and watched Miss Wilson with big, dark eyes. Not all of them had wanted to come; some were excited and glad to be there; but none was so passionate to learn as Janie.

In a few minutes Emma Wilson's skill had dispelled their fears, and they were playing games together, learning to be part of a social group. They were fashioning flower petals from colored paper, they were singing simple songs about Jesus' love for children, and somehow, in the midst of the fun, they were learning their letters.

All over the South the same thing was happening. Until the slaves were freed they had been forbidden to read and write, and teaching a slave his letters was a punishable act in many states. Then came freedom, and the deep, long-frustrated desire to learn burst forth. The desire was sadly misguided at first. Inhabitants of wretched cabins would possess huge books with impressive titles. The bigger the book and the longer the title, the better they loved it. Some lived on black-eyed peas, corn bread, and water, with no thought that a real education might teach them to eat better food. A young man would sit in the squalor of one room studying a French grammar or a Latin text, not realizing that what he must have first was a higher living standard and a trade.

Most of those earliest schools for Negroes were opened by Northern church missionary groups who launched a vast movement to end Negro illiteracy. Emma Wilson had been sent south by the Presbyterian Church. Trained at Scotia Seminary in Concord, North Carolina, she was better educated than most of the early teachers in the Negro South; and she hoped that her little handful of children would one day go out themselves as missionaries of learning. She worked tirelessly day after day the year around because of the dire need, although she knew that at the first sign of spring—and spring comes early in the South—many children would be snatched back to the fields.

The boys and girls came faithfully every day—well, almost every day; at any rate, Mary Jane McLeod never missed a day or an hour, or a minute. She covered the narrow dirt road at a fast clop-clop, and as the weather grew colder and the ground froze, her metal-toed brogans echoed on the hardened earth.

Sometimes Miss Wilson met her most faithful pupil at the door, held the cold hands in her own until they were limber and warmed, helped her out of her shawl and ill-fitting jacket, and allowed her to sit and rest before reciting.

Home Mary Jane walked when school was out, and each

evening the winter grew a little deeper and the day a little shorter until she was coming home in the dark. Huddled around the fire of pine chunks were her brothers and sisters.

"Hurry up, Janie! So we can eat supper!"

Mary trotted into the cabin, heading straight for her grandmother near the fireplace. The excited little girl flopped on the floor and leaned her head against the old lady's knees. Whenever she did that, Grandmother Sophia would lay a bony hand on her head, and that made her feel safe.

"Show us what you've learned!" cried the others, crowding around.

"Supper first," said Patsy. "Then we can all learn Mary's lesson."

That was how it happened every night. After supper was finished and the dishes washed, the entire McLeod family gathered about the most-learned scholar of them all while she imparted to them her brand-new knowledge. If she had lessons to prepare for the next day, she sat at the long table by the window, a candle or a smoky oil lamp her only light, and worked until bedtime.

The year flew by, and soon a supply of coarse yellow bricks was delivered to a vacant lot across the tracks from the railroad station, and a two-room building began to go up. Miss Wilson's dream of a school, Mayesville Institute, had materialized; for a long time to come, it would be the only school for the Negro children of Mayesville and the vicinity.

Mary Jane went that second winter to the two-room school, with Emma Wilson as teacher and the Reverend J. C. Simmons as pastor and principal. It was hardly comfortable, with an odd assortment of secondhand chairs and desks that never seemed to match the size of the student, a blackboard that was only a piece of cardboard painted over with black paint, a potbellied stove in the center of the room, filling the room with smoke whenever it was used; but teacher and children made it live. They decorated the windows with colored paper flowers; they hung their own art work on the walls; they lined the yellow-clay yard with whitewashed rocks; they hung rope swings from the trees.

The seasons went round again, and the letters of the alphabet lost their mystery as they were marshaled into words that could be recognized. The numbers from one to nine were no longer strange and terrifying but tools and instruments that could be put to work.

Mary McLeod became the center of her little community. *She* could count! Her neighbors—both white and colored—brought her their problems in arithmetic: the weight and price of their cotton, their debts at the village store, their percentage share of a crop.

"From the first, I made my learning, what little it was, useful every way I could," she wrote in later years. "Not until I had completed my schooling and had learned how to count and could study my father's bills and myself deal with the merchants to whom he was indebted were we able finally to lift the mortgage."

When a neighbor dropped by one evening and saw her with the Bible in her lap, he commented, "Sam's Mary reading the Blessed Book! Praise the Lord!"

Mary's position of leadership came to her quite naturally, for her parents were social leaders in their own right, probably because they were so industrious and hard-working. Many of the Negroes did not own their land, as the McLeods did, but were merely sharecroppers. That is, they worked the land for the owner on a profit-sharing basis, living in a cabin furnished by the absent white owner, and at the end of the season they accepted a share of the crop as pay for farming the land. The sharecroppers' cabins were wretched, unsanitary affairs, and the Negro who could not read and write was not always sure that he received his just reward after the cotton had been picked. He had to take what the white man was willing to give him. If it was enough to meet his debts, he felt lucky; too often it was not. Many Negro sharecropper families drifted from place to place, descending deeper and deeper into poverty.

The McLeods and a handful of others were an exception to the rule, and because they were so steady and reliable, others turned to them for strength. It was at the McLeod cabin that the neighbors were most apt to gather. Did Sam think the weather would hold up? Would Patsy give her recipe for dumplings? A woman down the road was having a baby (no doctors for Negroes); could Patsy or one of her older daughters please come and help?

The McLeods worked hard, too, in the Mayesville Methodist Church that stood on the dirt road near the railroad tracks, within sight of Emma Wilson's new school. Sunday morning saw the whole family, dressed in their best, start out on the five-mile trek. There was no work done on the Sabbath.

When the church was lucky enough to have an itinerant preacher for a while, he put up at the McLeods'. Then, indeed, the neighbors drifted in after supper, because there would be singing and gaiety and joyous worship. Poised in the open doorway, the minister would stand before his flock and stretch his arms over them in blessing, intoning the first lines of a hymn. The chorus of rich voices would join with his in one of America's most important kinds of folk music: the Negro spiritual.

The South Carolina moon shone bright overhead as they harmonized: "We are climbing Jacob's ladder," and Mary's strong contralto blended with the other voices.

Yes, she was climbing Jacob's ladder, she knew, as the scales of ignorance fell from her eyes; and she groped upward, upward.

October journeys are safest, brightest, and best.

"October Journey" by Margaret Walker

4. *One Glorious Morning*

The day came when Miss Wilson
had to tell Mary that she had no more to teach her. Mayesville Institute had given her all it could, and Mary's class
would graduate at the end of the term.

As a first graduation for her, a first for her classmates, and
a first for the Negroes of the Mayesville area, it was a grand
social event, and the McLeod family was not the only one to
arrive beaming with pride because one of its members had
brought it such an honor.

The students had built themselves a makeshift platform in
the school yard, decorating its sides with garlands of wild
greens gathered from the nearby swamps, arranging rows of
chairs before it to accommodate the graduating class and
guests. On that auspicious occasion Miss Emma Wilson sat on

the platform facing her charges, and on either side of her, in a prim row, were the guest speakers, both Negro and white, some of them members of the Board of the Presbyterian Church.

Patsy and Samuel found themselves seats as close to the front as possible, to watch the most important graduate of all: the twelve-year-old girl in the white dress, white shoes and stockings, who sat with her classmates a few rows ahead of them. Patsy herself had not been so decked out since her own wedding day. She wore a purple and white polka-dotted dress, brand-new black shoes, and a small-brimmed black straw hat. Her husband at her side had managed to assemble a whole suit, the parts of which were of varying colors and materials, and in his lap he carefully held a worn-at-the-edges beaver top hat.

Every graduating student recited, every guest on the platform made a speech, and at regular intervals the entire assembly punctuated the program with a song. At last came the presentation of diplomas, and each student had to walk to the platform when his name was called. The young man who was just ahead of Mary became so excited that he rushed forward, caught his toe on the top step, and sprawled on his face at Miss Wilson's feet. When her turn came, Mary arose with cast-iron calm, walked with great dignity to the platform, mounted the steps, received the precious roll of paper tied with a white satin ribbon, and returned to her place.

Unable to hear what followed once she had the treasure in her hand, Mary ran her fingertips affectionately along its edges. She had it at last—proof that she could read. Now if she picked up a book no one could insult her with the words, "*You* can't read!"

When benediction had been pronounced, families and friends crowded around the graduates. Congratulations! May we see your certificate? What beautiful letters!

Emma Wilson drew her most promising student aside and put an arm around her.

"What next for you, Mary?"

"I don't know, Miss Wilson. I want to go to school some more. Do colored folk ever go to college?"

"Not very often. Anyway, you would have to go to high school first."

Samuel overheard the conversation.

"We could pay a little money if the crop is good, and we could spare her if she wants more school," he offered.

"I'll see what I can do," Miss Wilson promised.

Almost a young woman, Mary returned to her life at the cabin and prayed for another divine miracle that would provide more schooling. There was no library for Negroes in Mayesville. There was nothing in Mayesville but endless stretches of cotton; and when plowing time came around again, she knew she would have to do her share in the field.

Spring brought an end to the dreaming, and each morning after she rolled off her straw-filled sacking, joined in the usual struggle at the tub on the back porch, and returned to the kitchen for breakfast, she went with her family for the long, hot day in the sun.

Down row after row they followed the mule, breaking the land for seed. The mule's head hung low and his big ears fell forward as though this was one plowing more than he could bear. His pace slowed, and neither the McLeod leading him nor the McLeod guiding the plow could increase his speed. At last, with most of the field still to be worked, Old Bush stopped and would go no farther. His eyes glazed over, his sides heaved, and he sank to the ground.

His worried owners gathered around him, trying to coax him to his feet. Samuel knelt down, lifted the furry head, and ran his hand under the muzzle and down the neck.

"Mule's dead," was his pronouncement.

Dead? The mule? They couldn't finish the plowing without him. If they couldn't plow, they couldn't plant or harvest. No crop meant starvation.

"Can we get another mule?" asked one, a little frightened by the tragedy.

"No money," Patsy explained. "No money until the cotton is picked."

But the cotton had not yet been planted!

Without prompting, they all knew that the situation must be faced. Weeping or moaning would do them no good. So they lifted the lifeless beast of burden, carried him to the edge of the field, and buried him. Then they all returned to the unplowed land. With a grim expression of fatality upon his young face, one of Samuel's sons stepped forward and took his place before the plow. Picking up the two straps of the harness and fitting them over his own shoulders, he bent forward and strained his full weight to the task. They would take turns pulling the plow, Samuel announced; it was too much for one.

The death of the mule meant the death of hope for Mary. She did not mind taking her turn at the plow; she was strong enough for that; but they would have to buy another mule, which would use up what little money was left over at harvest time. Even if an opportunity to go to school did arise, she would not be able to accept it. No school meant no life, no future.

"Lord, deliver me," she prayed. "Lord, help me go to school again, the way you did the last time."

The grim summer passed, and the cotton grew.

One day as Mary looked across the tops of the cotton shrubs she saw a familiar figure walking toward her, walking fast and waving an arm, as though she had news.

"Mary," called Miss Wilson, "I want to talk to you."

Mary was afraid to hope as she ran toward her beloved

teacher, whose face was radiant with happiness. Miss Wilson looked that happy only when she could bring joy to someone else.

"You want me, Miss Wilson?"

"I have such good news for you! A white lady out West has set up a scholarship for one student at our mission school, and you may have the scholarship."

"A white lady out West?" Mary asked incredulously.

A Mary Crissman in Denver, Colorado, a modest Quaker dressmaker, had decided to use her life's savings to help one Negro child toward more education, and Mary was to go to Scotia Seminary in Concord, North Carolina.

"Oh, the joy of that glorious morning! I can never forget it," is the way she herself told the story. "To this day my heart thrills with gratitude at the memory of that day. I was but a little girl, groping for the light, dreaming dreams and seeing visions in the cotton and rice fields, and away off in Denver, Colorado, a poor dressmaker, sewing for her daily bread, heard my call and came to my assistance. Out of her scanty earnings she invested in a life—my life!—and while God gives me strength, I shall strive to pass on to others the opportunities that this noble woman toiled and sacrificed to give me. How many self-denials she must have made! How many little legitimate pleasures she must have foregone, that the little black girl in South Carolina might have a chance. To me her memory is sacred! My earnest efforts for the hundreds of Negro girls in the Southland today are dedicated to the memory of this self-sacrificing woman who gave me my first real chance, and to the dear parents—father and mother—who so cheerfully gave me up, leaving them lonely and sad, while I prepared for my life's work."

That was the end of the cotton fields for Mary Jane, and a second time she sank down on her knees, stretched her hands to heaven, and gave thanks for deliverance.

Nothing ever moved slowly again. She must hurry, hurry, hurry to get ready for Scotia's fall term. This *was* the fall!

Excitement spread through the little community. Sam's Mary was going traveling! Everyone must hurry to be part of the honor that had come to Mayesville. Cabins were gay as hands knitted stockings for going-away gifts, or found a dress that could be made over to fit the scholar, or painstakingly stitched a ruffle on an apron. She must have everything that could be gathered together; she was everyone's pride and joy.

In the McLeod cabin even Grandmother became part of the happy commotion. She would take her pipe out of her mouth to give a piece of advice, only to find that she had to shout to make herself heard. Sam tried to speak, too, but it was no use; the women were running things. He would look at his sons hopelessly, and they would grin back their understanding. Laundering, mending, altering, knitting, packing did not come within their jurisdiction.

On departure day, precious little work was done for miles around, because everyone journeyed to the Mayesville station to see Mary Jane off to school.

"C'mon, c'mon!" Mary scolded her family. "I can't miss the train."

She stood nervously on the doorstep, waiting to start down the road. As they left the cabin—Sam, Patsy, Mary Jane, half a dozen brothers and sisters—a neighbor drove up with his farm wagon.

"Climb up!" he ordered. "You can't walk on such a day as this."

Into the wagon they clambered and rattled on to town, and as they went along others joined them, waving and calling from their cabins, calling to them to wait. The happy party grew bigger. When the wagon wheels jolted over the single pair of railroad tracks and turned down the road to the station, there were more jostling, joking, gossiping friends wait-

ing on the platform. Way up where the front car of the train
would stop they were herded, because Negroes had to ride in
the coach just behind the engine. The rest of the train was for
white folk.

As soon as the wagon drew to a stop Mary leaped out, because she had spotted Miss Wilson.

"Miss Wilson! Miss Wilson! Here I am!"

Miss Wilson held out her arms and caught the excited girl
to her.

"All packed and ready, I see," she laughed.

The crowd milled about its guest of honor.

A rumble and a puff of smoke in the distance announced
the arrival of the train, and Mary grabbed Miss Wilson's
hand for support. She had never been on a train before; she
had only watched them snort and wheeze past.

"Good-by! Good-by! Good luck at school."

Patsy gathered this strange and different child into her
arms for one last hug and started to cry.

"God bless my child," she pleaded as her voice thickened.

Sam could only turn his cap around in his hands and nod,
as the engine roared into the platform and drowned out everything that was said.

Some climbed aboard with Mary, carrying her bags and
bundles and seeing that she was settled in the seat.

"Good-by! Good-by! Learn all you can and come back and
tell us."

A shrill from the engine's whistle sent them rushing out of
the coach and down the steps.

"Good-by! Good-by!" Mary waved at them through the
dirty windowpane.

This was the end of something and the beginning of something else, she knew, as the train started to move.

She put her head back on the seat, closed her eyes, and
began to pray, "Please, dear Lord—"

For I am rightful fellow of their band.

"Mentors" by Gwendolyn Brooks

5. *First-Class Citizen*

Exhausted from the excitement and the train ride, dirty from the soft-coal soot, panicky at finding herself in a new environment for the first time in her life, Mary McLeod descended from the train at Concord, North Carolina, and stood beside her baggage on the gravel platform. The place was almost as rural as Mayesville, and the railroad station was scarcely any bigger. It had the familiar division through the middle, with two entrances to two waiting rooms: one marked "white" and the other "colored."

The only person around was a pleasant-looking white woman who was walking toward her, nodding and smiling as though she knew her.

"Are you Mary McLeod?" the white lady asked.

Mary jerked her head in the affirmative and wondered what it could mean. Why should a white person bother about her? She was going to Scotia Seminary, an institute for *Negro* girls.

"I've come to meet you and take you to Scotia," was the explanation; and Mary was to find that many of her teachers would be white. At Scotia she was to discover a different kind of white person, the kind who wanted the Negro to have a better opportunity to help himself.

Up a hill behind the railroad station and along a country road, the school was not far. With every step she took in her heavy brogans she felt firmer and firmer in her mission. She was going to learn and learn and learn and use every bit of her learning to help her own people. God had helped her with one miracle after another, and she would repay Him by living a life of service. Some day all Negroes would have a chance to go to school. Some day they would all be able to read the Bible. Some day . . .

A hand on her arm interrupted her daydream.

"Here it is," said her guide, pointing off to the right.

Set far back from the road, half hidden in a grove of giant shade trees, stood Graves Hall, a three-story brick building, its door graced by four white columns. To the right of Graves Hall stood a second building four stories tall, Faith Hall.

"Come," said the teacher, and together they started along the path to the entrance, and through the entrance to Mary McLeod's future.

Inside the doorway Mary stared in amazement, for before her were two sweeping flights of stairs with white risers and brown mahogany treads, one at her left hand and one at her right, joining in a balcony at the top. They seemed to go up forever, and Mary took a step backward. Never in her life had she climbed a flight of stairs!

"Your room is upstairs, Mary."

More from fear then courtesy, she waited for her escort to negotiate the upward journey ahead of her; then she followed suit, holding fast to the handrail as she ascended.

"And this is your room, Mary."

The frightened twelve-year-old looked popeyed at its neatness, its whiteness. There were two beds smoothly and tightly made up, one for herself and one for her roommate, two chests of drawers, two chairs, and two desks. That was all. There was none of the clutter of the McLeod cabin, that she had thought was a natural part of living. And the walls were of white plaster, a radical change from the knotty pine boards.

"Unpack your things and put them into the drawers of that chest," she was told. "Then wash your face and hands and come to the dining room. It is in the basement two flights down."

When the door closed and Mary was left alone, she looked at the zinc washbasin and the pitcher of water that stood in the center of it. A place to wash in—all her own!

Obediently she unpacked and tidied herself and started the perilous descent. A babble of voices led her toward the dining room, and with a quick little prayer she pushed the door open and stepped inside.

A sea of coal-black heads and brown faces turned to look, and the babble died away into a silence that was as quickly replaced by a wave of tittering and whispering and exchanging of amused glances. There she stood for her new world to see: no longer the reigning queen of Mayesville's cotton-picking community, but an ungainly, clumsy, rawboned field hand, poorly dressed and completely lacking in culture.

In the center of the room was the faculty table, and Mary received yet another shock when she saw Negro and white faculty members eating together. Mrs. Satterfield, wife of the school principal, left her place at the teachers' table and led Mary to her seat, introducing her to the dozen girls at her table and leaving her to their mercy.

The bewildered initiate looked hopelessly at the table before her. It was covered with a white cloth—her first tablecloth. On either side of her place were knife, fork, and spoon. She had never had one in her hand before, and she did not dare to ask about them for fear of being laughed at again. She could only copy the others. The first thing each did, after bowing her head to say grace, was to pick up the folded piece of cloth alongside of her place and lay it across her lap. Mary McLeod did the same. When she had been served with food, she reached furtively for the fork; but a sickish feeling of homesickness swept over her and she couldn't eat. This was all too much!

Homesickness did not mean giving up and going home. Mary was driven on by what she knew, even in those early days, to be her divine calling. Considering her misadventures, she made a remarkably quick adjustment to Scotia. Her generous nature, her willingness to laugh at her own mistakes, soon earned her friends among the more than three hundred schoolmates.

Her roommate, she found, was to be Abbie Greeley from Greensboro, North Carolina, who had already been at Scotia for two years and could take the new member under her wing, show her around, and with great pains help her to become accustomed to the surroundings and atmosphere. An enduring friendship developed between the two girls. Their philosophies were alike; both possessed the same high moral standards, the same religious fervor. They kept track of each other for years after they left Scotia. Abbie became a teacher and later married a Presbyterian minister and moved to Virginia to live.

Mary was willing to do any kind of work to remain at

Scotia. She labored in the school laundry, ironing Dr. Satter-field's shirts because she was so skillful with an iron; she cooked in the school kitchen, frequently winning a prize for a pie or cake or a feather-light loaf of bread. She was in charge of the school stairs, and in later years she could not resist the temptation to boast, "The stairs were always beautiful. The supervisor always gave me good marks on cleaning and scrub-bing and dusting and cooking. I realized that I had to do it well, because I was laying the foundation for a real life."

"Dick" McLeod, her classmates called her, because she was so strong and tireless.

Almost all the girls at Scotia had to do some kind of work to earn money toward their stay, but Mary's circumstances were probably more difficult than anyone's. The small schol-arship that Miss Crissman had given her met only a fraction of the total cost, and Mary had to earn almost her entire way. At one point she owned one shirtwaist, which she laundered each night and donned the next morning. Sometimes she was able to salvage garments from the missionary barrels.

A leader wherever she went, she soon became a leader among the girls at Scotia, organizing them into this and that, interceding for them with the authorities. She learned early how to go to the top person when she wanted something. One night when she was hungry she took her case to the head of the school, and Dr. Satterfield actually left his room, under the influence of her persuasion, and helped her hunt out some cheese and crackers in the kitchen.

Watching her Negro and white instructors mingle with one another and work together as equals was probably the finest experience that Scotia gave Mary. She had never met cultured Negroes before. They were gentle, educated, soft-spoken. Many of them were brown, not black like herself, and she wondered if she could ever be like them. Gradually a change took place within her, and she began to understand the meaning of equality. Scotia cleansed her of any last vestige of an inferiority complex. It transformed her from a second-class to a first-class citizen.

"The white teachers taught that the color of a person's skin has nothing to do with his brains, and that color, caste, or class distinctions are an evil thing. . . . I can never doubt the sincerity and wholeheartedness of some white people when I remember my experience with these beloved, consecrated teachers who took so much time and patience with me when patience and tolerance were needed."

Scotia Seminary, now Barber-Scotia College, was founded in 1867 by the Presbyterian Church. It was first housed in a frame two-story structure instead of the two brick buildings that Mary found when she entered. Twenty years after its founding, Dr. David J. Satterfield and Mrs. Nellie M. Satterfield came to Concord to handle the school, and it was their selfless and enlightened effort that wrought the change in Mary McLeod.

There were other white women at Scotia who, like the Satterfields, came there to work for twenty-five dollars a month and their board, when they could have found better teaching jobs elsewhere. Among them were Mary Chapman and Ida Cathcart, who both taught music.

The Negro women whom Mary found at Scotia had come to the school as rough and unpolished as she, and Dr. Satterfield had trained and educated them for their jobs, transforming them into teachers. Hattie Bowman, Miss Pegram, and Rebecca Cantey were among them.

When Miss Cantey's sister Cecelia, nicknamed "Teets," begged for a chance to go to Scotia, she was at first refused because she was too young. But the authorities relented finally and allowed her to come, feeling that an older sister on the faculty would be able to exert some control. It wasn't necessary, though, because Mary McLeod adopted the youngster almost at once, attending to her wants, holding her on her lap, rocking her when she cried; and another lifelong friendship had been created.

Scotia did even more for Mary than to give her dignity and friends: it helped her to discover her own talents. She had always known she could sing, but she hadn't realized how well, until she began to receive serious voice training in the school choir. Her contralto added depth and substance to their programs. Public speaking was another talent that came to light, and the school debating team learned to depend heavily upon her logical mind and her dramatic forcefulness.

She liked to make speeches about anything under the sun, and an outdoor sport at the school was to get Dick McLeod up on top of the rain barrel of Graves Hall so that she could harangue the throng.

The vigor with which she plunged into her studies startled the other students. They were there to learn, of course, but they felt no such desperation. Mary could do without food, but she was starved for learning. She must consume as much as possible, like a bear eating before hibernating, because it might have to do her for the rest of her life. The mysteries of algebra, the planned regularity of Latin grammar, the proper construction of a well-turned sentence in her own language; she needed it all.

Dr. Satterfield taught Bible, and he expected them to know the Book from cover to cover and their Catechism word for word. He was a severe teacher.

"I can see Dr. Satterfield's blue eyes piercing me right now," Mary McLeod laughed more than fifty years later.

When study and work allowed, she took long walks through the countryside. Concord was still in the cotton country. Cannon Manufacturing Company had one of its big mills there, with thousands of spindles and hundreds of looms consuming the bales of cotton. She had never before known where the cotton went that she helped to pick.

Concord was a small town then, its population a little over four thousand. On the main square the Concord National Bank and the St. Cloud Hotel were housed in a single three-story building. The only apparatus the fire department had was a horse-drawn reel of hose. Electric lights had been developed only recently and were regarded with some suspicion in the rural Carolinas.

Mary learned about tobacco and began to realize how many more crops America grew besides cotton.

There were ugly rumors of lynchings. A Negro who forgot to say "Sir" to a white man today might be dead tomorrow. The Ku Klux Klan became real to Mary, because she was older and her own horizons were widening. She overheard arguments about the wisdom of hiring colored labor in the cotton mills. Freed blacks were a problem in a town like Concord, because there were so many of them and because they wouldn't work unless they received pay for what they did. Money might not be good for them.

She realized that her own people had a history, and she delved into the few volumes in the Scotia library to find out more about the Negroes of America. Why were there Negroes in America? Why had there been slavery? Why had it been necessary to fight four years of civil war?

Kidnaped by traders, dragged away from their homelands and families, chained hand and foot in the stinking, rat-ridden holds of ships, many dying en route from abuse and starvation, Negroes were carried to the Western Hemisphere and sold for property. The slave trade had begun as far back as 1619, when a Dutch man-of-war brought twenty "negers" to Virginia.

Gradually slave trading became a profitable business. Many persons living in the New England states, who had no need to own slaves themselves, sent out ships to import human cargo—no questions asked—and sold the booty to the tobacco and cotton growers in the central and southern states. They considered this a perfectly respectable and dignified way to earn a living.

The tobacco growers were the first to use slaves in the fields, and in Virginia, where the climate was mild, the Negroes kept their health. When it was discovered how well rice would grow in the swamps of the Carolinas, the new crop created a demand for more cheap labor. But no one could survive the mosquito-ridden swamps, and the death toll kept the need for new importations of slaves running high.

The invention of the cotton gin in 1792 sent the demand for slaves skyrocketing upward, because cotton growers who had once produced a few thousand bales a year could now plant hundreds more acres and turn out millions of bales of cotton, shipping it to the mills in England and America. Cotton came into its own. Vast plantations developed, requiring more and more slaves to give cotton the hand cultivation it needed.

The fate of a slave was determined by the disposition of his master; to Mary, whose parents had had benevolent owners, knowledge of foul living conditions and the mistreatment endured by so many slaves, especially in the states farther south than Carolina, came as a shock. She read *Uncle Tom's Cabin* again and again, reliving the long, bitter struggle for the abolition of slavery.

The Civil War that had brought technical freedom also brought down upon the heads of both blacks and whites in the South the tragic years of revenge and reconstruction. The rush of cheap politicians into the South to exploit the bewildered, unprepared Negroes, the impoverishment that always follows a war, gave rise to the terrible race hatred which followed, to the Ku Klux Klan, to segregation and discrimination. The rule of the carpetbaggers was nearing its end when Mary was born in 1875, and she had been too young to understand. But her parents and older sisters and brothers had lived through it. When she returned to Mayesville, she would be able to learn more from them.

The summer after her first year at Scotia, Mary was not able to go home because of lack of funds, and that first summer was followed by five more when she worked during her free weeks as a cook, chambermaid, or laundress with one family or another in Pennsylvania and Virginia.

She spent seven years at Scotia, graduating at the end of five and remaining for two extra years of study: the "higher course." Scotia Seminary was the equivalent of a good high school and the "higher course" would have equalled junior-college work.

Those seven years wrought many changes in her thinking and personality. They gave her knowledge and vision and social training, although the learning was sometimes a little painful.

Bursting with good health and energy, she found it hard to remember to speak softly, and one day as she stood at the head of the double flight of stairs she saw someone in the lower corridor whom she recognized. "Ella!" she bellowed. "Hello, Ella!" Her voice echoed through the wooden corridors and brought President Satterfield out of his office.

"I shall have to give you a demerit for disturbing me," he announced.

Mary was mortified, because a demerit would be reported home to her family, and she begged him to take it off the record. Her mother and father would be deeply hurt, she told him, and she couldn't bear that. President Satterfield allowed her to worry about it long enough to make an impression, then he obligingly canceled the demerit.

Each Sunday morning during the school term Mary and her schoolmates attended worship in the Westminster Presbyterian Church, another red-brick, ivy-covered building surrounded by spreading shade trees, across the street from the Seminary. But Mary liked best the services in their own chapel in Faith Hall. They walked through a connecting vestibule and down two steps into the plain room with its polished floor and folding wooden chairs. The only light filtered through stained-glass windows at the sides of the room and the rose window behind the speakers' platform.

Here the girls quieted down voluntarily in the subdued light and spiritual atmosphere, as they bowed their heads in prayer or blended their voices in religious music. Mary's faith was replenished in those gatherings; her mission in life began to take on real substance. During her meditations she remembered the words of a Reverend J. W. E. Bowen who had once come to Mayesville Institute to lecture to the students. He had told them about Africa and the needs of the people there, and the zeal he had inspired in her childish heart then was reborn now as she stood on the threshold of adult life.

Was the returning memory of that lecture during her prayers a divine message? Mary thought so, and she determined to go to darkest Africa as a missionary. That would be her life of service.

She confided her ambition to Dr. Satterfield, who advised her to apply to Moody Bible Institute in Chicago for missionary training. He himself would write to the Presbyterian Board to inquire about the possibility of a scholarship.

That evening, with her departure from Scotia a little more than two weeks away, she sat at her desk on the second floor of Graves Hall and penned her letter of application to Moody:

Scotia Seminary
Concord, N.C.
May 26th, 1894

Miss L. L. Sherman:

It is my greatest desire to enter your Institute for the purpose of receiving Biblical training in order that I may be fully prepared for the great work which I trust I may be called to do in dark Africa. To be an earnest missionary is the ambition of my life.

I was born in Mayesville, South Carolina, July 10th, 1875. My educational advantages were very limited until I came to Scotia Seminary in 1887. I have been here since then and hope to graduate in the Scientific Course here June 13th, '94. My health has been, and is, very good. I shall hope to be able to enter the Institute sometime in July and take the course necessary for my work.

Very truly yours,
MARY J. McLEOD

When she had finished the momentous letter, she left her desk and sat on the edge of her bed. Sliding her hand under the pillow, she brought out a treasure, the small end of a stick of peppermint candy. Candy was probably the only luxury she allowed herself during the entire seven years at Scotia. With money so hard to come by, the purchase of a stick of peppermint was a rare treat, and she made it last a long time, hiding it under her pillow to avoid being tempted by the sight of it, breaking off a tiny piece at a time.

With high hopes for the future, she popped the last fragment of candy into her mouth.

Our song has filled the twilight
and our hope has heralded the dawn.

"We Have Been Believers" by Margaret Walker

6. *Singing Missionary*

The excited twelve-year-old girl who had boarded her first train at Mayesville station, wearing pigtails and loaded with bundles, was no more. Seven years later a prim nineteen-year-old stepped down from the train on her first visit back home. The ill-fitting homemade clothes had been replaced by a stylish, if threadbare, shirtwaist and skirt, and the hair was brushed back in a pompadour. Her shoes, still heavy and serviceable, were no longer decorated with the protective metal tips, and her belongings were concealed in a pasteboard traveling case.

This new young woman, so completely remade, so filled with righteous intent, looked about her after the train pulled out and saw Mayesville in a different perspective. There was the little frame church in need of a coat of paint, flanked on either side by Negro shanties, and there on the other side of the tracks was Mayesville Institute. A new dormitory building had been put up near the two-room structure where she had studied. It was almost as small as the original and looked as though it was as cheaply equipped inside.

She walked slowly along the gravel path to the road. In the distance she could see the large homes of the white folk and the handsome building in which their children were educated. She turned right, crossed the railroad tracks, and started the dusty five-mile walk that she remembered so well. " 'Let my people go. Let them go,' " she hummed the familiar tune. " 'Tell old Pharoah . . .' "

The rattle of wagon wheels and the clop-clop of hoofs made her turn her head. The wagon drew to a stop alongside of her, and the driver nodded, offering her a lift. Mary recognized the leathery brown face of a neighbor.

"Don't you remember me?" she laughed as she climbed up into the seat beside him.

The man was obviously bewildered.

"I'm Mary Jane McLeod, back for a visit."

"Sam's little Mary? Why, child! How you've grown!"

Joyously he whipped up his horse, and the bony beast lunged forward in a slow lope as though he, too, had caught the excitement. The driver grinned and laughed. Sam's Mary back home! And he was the first to know. His would be the privilege of telling everyone the glad tidings.

The news spread like wildfire. Ceaseless toil stopped as hoes were laid down, mules tethered, crab grass deserted, and Mayesville's Negro community converged upon the McLeod cabin to welcome home its favorite. In the midst of the joyous commotion Mary tried to explain that she was not home to stay.

"Just a few weeks," she said. "I'm going to Moody Bible Institute in Chicago."

She had already learned that she had been granted another scholarship by Miss Mary Crissman, and she told family and neighbors of her great dream to go as a missionary to Africa and help black folk there. They weren't surprised; they had always known she was destined to do something great and noble.

Mary made the most of those few weeks in Mayesville. She held classes three evenings a week for anyone who wished to come, one of those evenings devoted to literature and music. The little Sunday school perked up and took on new life. She worked tirelessly all the time she was home to give family and friends some fragment of the learning she possessed.

Another departure day with its tearful farewells had to be faced, and Mary set out on the long, long journey to Chicago, a city so large and so far away that it existed only in her wildest imaginings.

She was met at the Chicago terminal by a group from Moody, all of them white; and when she reached the school she found that, except for one African student, she was the only Negro in the school. She alone represented her people in this new community, and all Negroes everywhere would be judged by her conduct. She was not the only "colored" person there by any means; Moody was training Japanese, Chinese, and Indian missionaries as well. Her roommate was to be Anna Thompson from Logansport, Ohio—white—but thanks to Scotia, Mary no longer felt any suspicion toward white folk.

"There were no feelings of race at Moody," she recorded. "There we learned to look upon a man as a man, not as a Caucasian or a Negro. My heart had been somewhat hardened. As the whites had meted out to me, I was disposed to measure to them; but here, under this benign influence, including that of Dwight L. Moody, a love for the whole human family, regardless of creed, class, or color, entered my soul and remains with me, thank God, to this day."

Dwight L. Moody, the dramatic and eloquent evangelist, who founded Moody Bible Institute, was a man of fifty-seven when Mary McLeod came under his guidance. He stood tall and erect in the pulpit; heavily built, with a short white beard, his vest buttoned snugly over a bulging stomach, he would hold his Bible open in his left hand as he gestured and emphasized with his right and spoke commandingly of his text. He was a world figure and had been on speaking tours in Europe as well as America. Wherever he went, crowds flocked to hear him; they filled the great opera house in London when he was there and surged through the streets of Edinburgh.

At Moody, Mary received more musical training with Dr. Charles Alexander and sang in the choral group under Dr. D. B. Towner twice a week. Every Thursday found her at the police station singing to the prisoners, talking with them, giving them literature. She spent her lunch hours at the Pacific Garden Mission, where she served food to drunks and street people who were brought in.

This was real! This was service! Mary was in the work she loved best, the work she wanted always to do.

Field service was part of the training for Moody's students, and Mary McLeod's enthusiasm reached the bursting point when she was allowed to venture into Chicago's slums and call on the needy in their homes.

Wandering about in that city was an adventure in itself. Chicago had busy street after busy street with horses and carriages whipping by. It had office buildings sixteen stories high. Almost all of Chicago was new, because the entire city had been destroyed by fire a little more than twenty years before, when a tipped-over lamp in a shanty had turned the old city of frame buildings and wooden sidewalks, tinder-dry after a long drought, into a mass of flames.

Lincoln and Douglas had debated the slavery issue in this city, and Illinois was Abraham Lincoln's home state. Chicago had been a station on the Underground Railroad, the system for smuggling slaves out of the South into Canada.

Out the intrepid daughter of slaves stepped on her newest, most exciting assignment.

"I started out on Monday morning, my heart beating high with love and the desire for service. The world seemed so beautiful as I stepped out of the Institute, our morning hymn still on my lips, our morning lesson—'The Lord is my light and my salvation,' nerving me to earnest efforts. Into house after house I went, carrying God's message, sometimes to the sick, sometimes to the discouraged, again to the sorrowing. In one house the light of the home had gone out—the little baby daughter, the only child, lay cold and still in death. It was a privilege to clasp that mother's hand and assure her that Jesus cared, and that not a sparrow falls without His notice.

"In another lowly home an old man nearly ninety had learned to know me and to look for my coming to sing to him and read God's word. He was nearly blind and very feeble, but his faith was strong, and I really derived more benefit from the visit then he did.

"With my heart aglow with love, my spirit lifted, I passed to my next assignment."

As the young enthusiast climbed the stairs of the next tenement and knocked on the door, sounds of drunken revelry reached her ears through the thin wooden panel. She turned to run, but it was too late. The door opened upon a small room crowded with men and women playing cards and drinking. A huge, unkempt man, his eyes glassy, grabbed Mary's arm and dragged her into the room. He closed the door, locked it, and put the key in his pocket, bellowing to the crowd:

"This is the missionary lady! Well, honey, you're a mighty good little saint but you'll sure drink one glass of beer today!"

"I don't touch it," she whispered faintly.

They roared with laughter and began to jeer, "She's too good! But we got her now! She'll drink the beer or stay here all night."

" 'Whom shall I fear?' " Mary whispered the gospel words, and aloud she said, "I am a Christian woman. I am about my Master's business and I have no fear. God will take care of me. Please open the door at once."

When she realized that they were not going to release her, she sat down, gathered all of her courage, and began to chat. As well preach the gospel here as elsewhere.

"What are you doing? Going around and converting people?" asked one.

"No," she explained. "I can't convert people. I am just trying to expose them to things that will lead them to think about the best for themselves."

They laughed.

"Won't you have a glass of beer?"

"No, but I would like a glass of water."

She rose to go, but one of the men spoke. "You are going to stay right here. The key is in my pocket."

She just sat and breathed a prayer, enduring their jeering and comment for a quarter of an hour.

"Will you kindly let me out?" she asked.

"No, you are going to stay here."

Then she stopped asking and just sat quietly. Darkness was coming on, and she could tell that her captors were beginning to feel disturbed.

Finally one of the women stood up and said, "Now, listen;

Miss McLeod is doing a work that is helpful to all people. She is doing something that is helpful to us if we have sense enough and courage enough to abide by what she says. This woman is very young. I have sisters, and I have been a girl myself, and I am not going to tolerate this any longer. Open that door and let her out."

"Where do you come from?" someone asked Mary.

"South Carolina."

"Do you have any sisters and brothers?"

"Yes, I have sixteen. My mother and father were slaves."

"I don't know anything about slavery and I don't care about it, but do you hope to break up a place like this by going around doing what you are doing?"

"I don't know," Mary answered truthfully. "But I hope the things we are trying to do, the literature we are leaving for people to read, and the talks we are giving, will help to lead people out of places like this."

While she talked, the key to the door was produced and the door unlocked for her.

"Moody is a good distance from here, and it's dark by now. Are you afraid to go by yourself?"

"No."

"Well, I think we've teased you long enough. I think there are very few people in the world like you. You're wonderful. I hope you will do some good. I hope some day I may have sense enough to know what you are talking about."

Mary hurried out of the door and down the stairs; she took a cab back to the Institute, feeling it would be wiser than a streetcar at that hour. She found the school wild with worry because she hadn't come in for dinner.

"I wasn't afraid," she assured them. "I knew I had protection."

In the northern and middle-western states a Negro was often a curiosity, and when Mary went out in the Gospel Car

—a railroad coach that cruised through the neglected areas—
to establish Sunday schools and church centers, with five or six
of her schoolmates, to preach and sing hymns, her coal-black
skin attracted attention. A seasoned gambler once came forward from the crowd and declared his faith after "hearing the
colored girl sing."

When they were as far west as the Dakotas, the missionary
group was put up overnight in the home of a minister and his
wife. The couple had a five-year-old daughter who had never
seen a Negro before. She loved Mary McLeod immediately, as
all children did, and they played together until dinner time.

When the meal was ready the mother said, "Miss McLeod,
will you come in and have dinner?"

"Mother!" cried the startled child. "Tell the lady to wash
her face and hands. She's all dirty."

Mortified by the child's rudeness, the parents started to
apologize, but Mary smiled. "I am not at all ashamed of my
color. I'm proud of my black skin."

Then she lifted the little girl up on her lap and allowed
her to touch her skin, even rub it, to learn that the color would
not come off.

"Look; my skin is just like your skin. It stays the way God
made it."

She took a vase of flowers from a nearby stand and held it in
front of her.

"Look at all the different colors of these flowers," she spoke
on. "God made men just the way he made the flowers, some
one color, some another, so that when they are gathered together they make a beautiful bouquet."

Tears coursed down the mother's cheeks as she listened,
and when the story was finished she said, "Miss McLeod, if
you came out here to do nothing else but give my child that
lesson, your journey has warranted your coming."

Mary's poise seemed to be adequate for any situation that

confronted her. She could meet the unexpected frank comment of a small child, the confusion and noise of a big city, good news or bad, with the same steadiness with which she had mounted the graduation platform of Mayesville Institute to accept her first diploma.

When she received a letter from Mayesville, opened it, read it, and walked quietly to her room, no one could have guessed from her dignified bearing that the letter contained bad news, extremely bad news. The McLeod cabin had burned to the ground. The unpainted, splintery dry pine somehow had caught fire; perhaps a spark had escaped from the fireplace or from a crack in the flue of the ungainly old kitchen stove; and the flames had shot skyward, licking the walls and wrapping the little home in a hot blanket of destruction before anything could be done. This meant increasing the mortgage on the land and on future cotton crops to buy material for a new cabin and its contents. The family had to have a roof over its head, even though it meant debts, debts, debts to the end of time.

Mary felt helpless in the face of this new woe. There was nothing she could do, really, except pray for another divine miracle. Negroes had to face so many discouraging odds and so much hopelessness.

She went on about her studies and her missionary tasks, for the end of the year was almost at hand, and she must pass her final examinations well if she was to deserve an appointment to Africa. She knew she was ready for it. Her stay at Moody had strengthened her religious faith and had given her priceless experience.

When she received word to report to the school's reception room, she hurried through the corridors, hoping for news of an appointment. She found a group of ladies waiting to meet her, but they were not from any mission board. They had heard her beautiful voice, and they wondered if she would consent to sing before a group of friends—rather a large affair. Mary McLeod, the kind, the generous, the cheerful, never let them know how they had disappointed her; and she consented to sing at their gathering.

To her surprise, a few days later, she recieved a letter from them, and when she opened it a check for the handsome sum of forty dollars fluttered out. In 1895, forty dollars was worth many times more than it is today. Without the slightest hesitation Mary endorsed the check, popped it into another envelope, and mailed it to her parents. It would go a long way toward rebuilding the cabin that had been destroyed by fire.

As soon as graduation day was over, she traveled to New York to ask the Presbyterian Board of Missions for a station in Africa. The Mission Board members shook their heads at the twenty-year-old. There was no opening for a Negro in Africa at that time.

"The greatest disappointment of my life," she described it. "Those were cruel days."

With crushed hopes and a heavy heart she accepted a teaching assignment at Haines Normal Institute in Augusta, Georgia.

The soft gray hands of sleep
Toiled all night long
To spin a beautiful garment
Of dreams.

"Forgotten Dreams" by Edward Silvera

7. *Serving and Waiting*

Mary knew she had left Abraham Lincoln's state behind and that she was back in the South-land once more. Georgia was especially hard on its Negro population, with its chain gang for prisoners, its Jim Crow laws, and its segregation. In this state the letters K.K.K. had a grim meaning. In fact, Georgia had always been severe with its Negroes; slaves had been so cruelly treated—beatings, maimings, evil food—that the whites lived in constant fear of slave revolts. One plot to destroy the city of Augusta had been uncovered just in time, and another plan to murder the whites of Savannah was defeated.

Augusta, on the Savannah River which separates Georgia from South Carolina, is an old city that began as a fortress be-fore the American Revolution. It had escaped the worst burning and pillage of the Civil War, and when Mary moved there to take her first teaching post, she found some of its oldest landmarks still standing. Just two miles south of Augusta, on Rocky Creek, Eli Whitney had built his first cotton gin. In and about the city Mary heard the whir and hum of Georgia's cotton textile mills, and she watched the steam packets, freighters, and shallow-water craft come up the sleepy Savannah River as far as Augusta, bringing baled cotton to the mills, carrying away the woven fabric.

She found the Negroes of Augusta crowded into a section called "The Terry," living in the familiar unpainted shacks along unpaved streets that were clouds of dust when dry and mud traps when wet.

In the midst of the squalor stood Haines Normal Institute, a four-story brick building on Robert and Gwinnett Streets, the newly realized dream of its guiding spirit and founder, Lucy Laney.

Lucy Laney, twenty years older than Mary McLeod, had been born in slavery but to a life less cruel than that of many Georgia slaves, for her parents had been allowed to live together after their marriage and had worked in the big house instead of in the fields. Lucy was taught to read and write by her mother's owner and was allowed the freedom of a huge library while her mother cleaned the room.

Fired with a desire to bring education to her people, she was ready to enter Atlanta University at fifteen. A few years of teaching in Savannah convinced her that she wanted a school for Negro children in Augusta, where one was most needed, and she asked the Presbyterian Board of Missions for Freedmen for aid. They blessed her with their approval but gave no financial support.

Lucy Laney went to work anyway, beginning in the basement of a church. Finding children for her school was no problem, but finding among the ragged and dirty urchins enough children who could pay her a few cents a week tuition was another matter. Miss Laney managed, and by the end of the second year she had two hundred and thirty-four pupils, many of them boarding with her, and she moved to a large, deserted house and barn she had been able to rent cheaply because it was supposed to be haunted.

The Presbyterian Mission Board was so impressed with her report that it allocated $10,000 to her school, and during the third year a well-to-do visitor from the North donated a piece of land and another $10,000 to erect the brick school in which Mary McLeod went to work in 1895. The main building had classrooms on the first floor and dormitory rooms for girls on the upper floors, while the boys boarded in nearby cottages.

When the slim, strong Mary McLeod clasped hands with the short, rotund Lucy Laney, a deep friendship was born, and Mary's disappointment at not being able to go to Africa lost some of its sting. She found in Miss Laney's tireless effort and utter disregard for herself a new inspiration. She could look at the corridors teeming with happy children who had been gathered up, washed up, and guided into better lives, and realize that she was needed here, too.

"Her school was a torchlight there in its community," was the younger woman's comment. "Still, around it there were hundreds and hundreds of people who were not touched. I roomed on the third floor, and I could look out of my window into the alleyways of The Terry and see masses of unkempt children, just trying to find their way as best they could."

Mary McLeod possessed so much vitality and natural enthusiasm that her spirits could not be kept down long, and she plunged into teaching with the same vigor and intensity with which she did everything.

"It was a delight to note the real enthusiasm with which Miss McLeod entered upon her work," said one who knew her in those days.

Lucy Laney understood the ambitious young woman's feeling of frustration and did all she could to comfort her.

"She helped me see that Africans in America need Christ and school just as much as Negroes in Africa."

Mary McLeod could never look at dire need without doing something about it, and she went straight to Miss Laney.

"These children out in the streets need a Sunday mission school," she said, and the wise Miss Laney nodded her approval.

A nod of encouragement was all Mary needed, and she went into the alleys and back streets, taking her eighth graders with her for aides, and invited these children of the streets to come to Haines on Sunday afternoons. She gathered every bedraggled urchin who could be persuaded—the number eventually ran to a thousand—organized them into a choral group, sang hymns with them, taught them Bible stories, gave them religious tracts to take home.

Other social workers in the city were attracted by the phenomenon, and they joined in teaching at the mission school. The faculty and upper-class students helped Miss McLeod collect clothes, soap, toothbrushes, combs, pins, towels, and knocked at the door of each child's home to preach the gospel of cleanliness. Wherever they called, the day was a little brighter and the future a little more hopeful.

"I can never forget her," said a Y.M.C.A. worker friend of hers. "I was at Miss Laney's school when she taught there. Her glorious voice and her rare missionary spirit drew everyone to her. Oh, how she could sing! It was a joy to hear her and an inspiration to touch her glowing life."

Miss McLeod's "glowing life" reached beyond Augusta, all the way back to Mayesville; for when she drew her first pay check she sent the greater portion of it to her father so that he could start paying off the mortgage on the cabin. Her parents were going to have a better home some day, as soon as she could earn enough money; and eventually she was able to buy them a little house in Sumter, North Carolina, a short distance from Mayesville, a place with plastered walls, sparkling glass windows, running water, a living room and bathroom, and a porch. Her mother and father spent their last years in the Sumter house, with comfortable beds, plenty of linen, and their youngest child to care for them—Hattie, the one who had been a nursing infant when Mary had worked in the fields.

Miss McLeod was not destined to remain so far away from home for very long, and the next teaching assignment she received from the Presbyterian Board was in Sumter, at Kindell Institute, another church-supported school for Negroes.

During her two years at Kindell she kept almost nothing for herself, sending home her salary to pay off the mortgage and to help two of her sisters through Scotia. Her family sent her rice and meal so that she would have enough to eat, and in her off hours she did light housekeeping for extra money.

Not all of Mary McLeod's day was devoted to the somber side of life, to self-sacrifice and hard work. She was an attractive young lady, with more than a fair share of suitors. She liked the company of young men, and they sought her out, presenting a highly polished apple, a baked potato, or whatever they could afford; but they seldom measured up to her standards, nor could they match her missionary zeal. Estella Roberts, who lived with her, the daughter of a Presbyterian minister, was one of her fellow teachers, and Estella determined to find a man who could qualify.

The two women had become fast friends at Kindell—both assigned there to teach, both joining the Presbyterian Church and singing in the choir.

One day a tall, handsome young man appeared at choir practice as a new tenor of the group and seated himself in the front row. The scheming Estella took one look and made it her business to meet him that same evening, promptly introducing him to Mary.

"Mary, dear, this is Mr. Albertus Bethune," she said with emphasis, and proceeded to drag information about himself from the young man. He had been a student at Avery Institute of Charleston, but he hadn't finished college because he wanted to work at a dry-goods store in Sumter to help his brother through college.

"I am planning to go to Africa as a missionary as soon as I can obtain an assignment," Mary McLeod announced, lest any far-fetched notions pop into his head.

Estella had decided otherwise, and she would not be defeated. She arranged situations so that the two would be brought together, encouraging first one and then the other. Albertus Bethune needed little encouraging, and within a few months he was irrevocably in love with the vivacious, ambitious lady with the beautiful singing voice. He would rather have died than miss choir practice.

Estella was thrilled, and she carried her plans still further. The horseless carriage had not yet come into vogue, and bicycles were all the rage. She decided that Miss McLeod should learn to ride a bicycle and that Mr. Bethune should teach her.

Mary, who at first had briefly and flatly spurned the attentions of this man, began to look forward to his company and finally consented to his friendship. By the time she had mastered the art of riding a bicycle, her interest had deepened into love, and during her second year at Sumter Mary McLeod and Albertus Bethune were married in the Presbyterian parsonage at Sumter by the Reverend J. C. Watkins, under whom Mary had been teaching. Her older sister Margery came home from Scotia to attend the wedding.

The bride and groom set out to make a home in Savannah,

Georgia, where he had a teaching assignment. There they could afford only a small apartment in the home of Mrs. Ella Lee on Robert Street—sitting room, bedroom, and bath, with the privilege of using the kitchen downstairs—for teachers in the South were paid small salaries and Negroes were paid even less.

Estella's father, Reverend Doctor Roberts, had a church in Savannah, and he called on the Bethunes often. So did Miss Irene Smallwood (later Mrs. J. W. E. Bowen), who had taught kindergarten at Lucy Laney's school.

Mary McLeod Bethune had thought that she would be able to find a teaching position in Savannah to supplement their meager income, but when she learned that she was to have a child of her own, all her plans changed. She would stay home and be a full-time mother!

For the first few months after Albert McLeod Bethune was born, all of Mary Bethune's time was taken up with caring for her infant son, but having a child of her own did not make her want to stay at home; instead, she felt a deeper concern for all children. She began to worry about Albert's education, his future, his opportunities. Would the world have anything to offer this Negro child unless she herself created his chances?

The Reverend Eugene Ugams, of Palatka, Florida, was visiting at the house then, paying court to Irene Smallwood, and it looked as though the couple would be married. The Bethunes, Irene, and the Reverend Ugams used to sit around in the evenings talking over the future, and a plan grew out of the conversations. They would all go to Palatka and start a school.

That plan never materialized, largely because Irene Smallwood and the Reverend Ugams did not marry after all, but Mary Bethune could not rest. Her year with Lucy Laney had proved to her what could be done with sufficient faith and fortitude. She wanted to found a school of her own.

Each time she closed her eyes in prayer she asked fervently for guidance, for an opportunity to realize her wish, for a clue to the future. One night, after she had tossed about, unable to sleep, thinking about all the children who needed help, she at last fell into a fitful slumber and began to dream.

In her dream she found herself wading out into an ocean; on one side of her was Dr. Satterfield and on the other side her mother and father. They had her locked in their arms, supporting her as they waded out into the deep. Soon her father said, "This is as far as I can go; the water is getting very deep. I shall have to go back. Do the best you can, Mary."

"Thank you, Papa," said Mary.

After her father had left, they waded on out, until her mother said, "Daughter, I have done all I can. This is as far as I can go with you. I must return."

"Thank you, Mama. I will do my best."

The water rose higher around Mary and Dr. Satterfield. At last it was Dr. Satterfield's turn to say, "Mary, I cannot go beyond this point. I have done all I can do. You will have to make it to the other shore alone. Good-by."

Left to face a great expanse of trackless water without a single guiding hand, Mary awoke with a start. What was it she must face alone? Her parents and Dr. Satterfield had given her all the aid at their command, and they had urged her to go on.

She *would* go on! The consuming drive that burned within her would not let her rest. She must return to teaching; she must work for Negro children; she must found a school of her own. Although the baby was only nine months old, she persuaded her husband to let her go to Palatka and take a teaching post in a mission school there. It would give her an opportunity to find out whether Palatka was the place for her school.

Albertus Bethune was never as interested as his wife in education. To him it was a way to earn a living, and he couldn't understand that her soul was on fire.

"You are foolish to make sacrifices and build for nothing. Why not stop chasing around and stay put in a good job?" he would say.

He allowed her to depart for Florida, feeling certain that she would soon become discouraged and return to Savannah.

She rented a cottage on Lemon Street in Palatka, found a former friend in town who would care for her baby during the day, and took up her teaching duties.

The lad of ten, Leroy Bazzell, whose task it was to mind the Bethune baby, adored the lady who stopped at his mother's house every morning on the way to her school, had breakfast with them, and left her young son to his care. The baby Albert wasn't very much trouble, he decided, and didn't interfere too much with his own childish interests.

The school had been limping along on the verge of failure until Mrs. Bethune arrived and electrified it with her personality, her enthusiasm and imagination. So many children on the streets who needed to be helped! So many dirty, unruly youngsters growing up like little animals in the crowded, unsanitary slums assigned to Negroes. Every town in the Deep South seemed to tell the same story, with the railroad track dividing the town between black and white. In a short time the school had been reorganized, children were flocking in, and the Presbyterian Board had to send three more teachers to handle the crowd.

Once she had her school running smoothly, Mary McLeod Bethune looked about for more work to fill her leisure time. Palatka was the county seat, she learned, and it had a jail full of lost souls. So every Thursday and Sunday she visited the prisoners, sang hymns, talked with them, told them Bible stories, and persuaded them to tidy their persons. She was greeted with jeers at first, but gradually the scorn of those hardened men dissolved, and they began to look forward to her visits. Even the jailer would say, "Come, boys, clean up, spruce up, your missionary will be here today." For three years she never failed them. She even succeeded in having one man released when she learned that he had been convicted on a false charge.

One night in Palatka Mary Bethune had another dream.

She was recovering from a touch of grippe and still had a fever; even in her sleep she turned her head from side to side, trying to feel cooler and breathe more easily. In her dream she was standing at the edge of the St. John's River, and again she had the feeling that she must cross. Just as she was about to step into the water, a man who was standing by with a boat came up to her and said, "Look ahead of you."

She looked, and he asked, "What do you see?"

She saw a great array of boys and girls, all uniformed, the girls in white middies and blue skirts and the boys in dark suits. There seemed to be thousands of them.

"I see a great army of young people," she told her interrogator.

At her side she noticed a table with a large ledger opened, and the man spoke again: "You see that array of young people?"

"Yes."

"You will have to register the names of every single one of them in this ledger before I can take you across."

Awake at once, Mary Bethune sat up in bed, her head aching and throbbing, her pulse racing with excitement. Thousands and thousands of young people, the man had said. She must go on! Palatka was not for her! She must go on searching until she found the army of young people who needed her so desperately.

Her letters to her husband in Savannah were full of the excitement and yearning that she felt, and he realized that she would never come back; so he joined her in Palatka.

She went about her duties—teaching, visiting the prison— still searching for a school of her own. Whenever she had a few dollars to spare, she would spend it on train fare to visit some nearby point where she had heard there was need of a school. None satisfied her. She even worked as an insurance collector to obtain a little more money.

Word reached her that Flagler was building the Florida East Coast Railroad as far as Miami and that Negro day laborers were congregating all down the coast along the site of the construction, living without leadership or restraint, almost like wild creatures.

That might be the answer!

Bundling up her son, who was not yet five years old, and a few personal effects, she set out for Daytona Beach. When she stepped from the crowded, littered Jim Crow coach at Daytona and started to walk along the railroad platform, she saw that conditions were even worse than she had been warned to expect. The Flagler interests were using Negro labor because it was cheap, and what money the workmen did recieve was spent on hard liquor, gambling, and carousing. They lived in a squalor no better than the worst days of slavery.

Mary McLeod Bethune walked on, away from the line of construction toward the shore, where the Halifax River flowed south along the coastline, cutting off a long, narrow peninsula of land on which an occasional solitary home of some wealthy resorter stood carefully isolated from its neighbors, ignoring the confusion of the Negro quarters on the land side of the river.

The river glistening like silver in the sun, the palmettos and evergreen oaks hung with moss, the low rolling hills—incredibly beautiful!

She strolled back to Colored Town and stood in the midst of the human exploitation. Deep down inside of her a voice seemed to say, "This is the spot. This is the place for your school."

It is dangerous for a woman to defy the gods;
To taunt them with the tongue's thin tip,
Or strut in the weakness of mere humanity,
Or draw a line daring them to cross.

"Letter to My Sister" by Anne Spencer

8. *On a Public Dump Heap*

Mary McLeod Bethune had $1.50 in her pocket and no place to spend the night, and she looked anxiously at the setting sun. She knew a family here; perhaps they would shelter her and her son.

Her friend, a Mrs. Warren, still lived at the same address and gladly invited her to stay with them until she was able to make other arrangements. She talked to them excitedly all through dinner. She was going to found a school for Negro girls! They shook their heads. It was not a good idea, they advised her; Negroes who forgot their place only brought trouble upon their own heads. The Klan was active down here.

"I know all about that," she replied. "I've been living just a few miles north of here in Palatka. I think it is time the

Negroes did something to better their own conditions instead of waiting for whites to allow it."

"You don't realize how bad conditions are here," said one Negro after another. "Please don't stir up any trouble."

Mrs. Bethune held her peace, because she had known that as many Negroes as whites would be opposed to her plan. The next morning, taking young Albert by the hand, she started out with Mrs. Warren, trudging from door to door. Accepting rebuff and insult as inevitable, she kept on without discouragement, seeking a building, a cottage, a shack, any available place in which to begin her school.

"If you're smart enough to teach, why don't you take examinations and teach in the public schools?"

"White folk'll say you're educating the Negroes clean out of their place, and they won't want to be servants any more."

On Oak Street, an unpaved lane only three blocks long, lined on either side with jerry-built hovels, she turned in at number 529, because she had been told that the owner, John H. Williams, would be willing to rent the place.

He was sitting in a rocking chair on the porch when Mary McLeod Bethune walked up the path and explained her ambition.

"I can rent it to you for eleven dollars a month," he agreed.

When she admitted that she did not have that much money with her and would not have it until she could find a way to earn it, he smiled and nodded. There was something about her candid manner that made him say, "All right, I'll trust you for the rent. You may have the cottage."

The Oak Street cottage had four tiny rooms downstairs and a narrow porch across the front. There were three rooms upstairs, which Mrs. Bethune used for her living quarters. A sulphur well in the cellar furnished water; kerosene lamps provided light; and a toilet stood in the back yard.

Nothing could stop her now! Daytona was teeming with

Negro children; she had a place for them, and she had her
health and her faith in God. What more could possibly be
needed?

"Mama, Papa, Dr. Satterfield, Dwight Moody, Lucy Laney,
I haven't forgotten any of you! Your training hasn't been
wasted."

She worked at a furious pace getting the cottage ready so
that her school could open in October, only a month after
her arrival. With the help of sympathetic neighbors, she
combed the dump heaps and refuse piles behind the resort
hotels for cracked dishes, broken furniture, and bits of cloth.
She went from one back door to another, begging for a broom,
a lamp, discarded linen, or a few pennies. She burned logs
and used the charred pieces for pencils, and boiled down
elderberries to make ink. Boxes and inverted baskets served
as chairs, and a large packing box was her desk.

"Everything was scoured and mended. This was part of the
training: to salvage, to reconstruct, to make bricks without straw," was her own brief comment.

She baked sweet-potato pies and sold them to the workmen
along the railroad tracks to supplement her income, and she
canvassed the peninsula side of town one day a week for cash
donations for her school.

On October 3, 1904, Daytona Educational and Industrial
Training School for Negro Girls, Mary McLeod Bethune,
Principal, was officially opened with five little girls aged from
eight to twelve and one little boy, Albert McLeod Bethune.
The parents of the girls had agreed to pay fifty cents a week
tuition.

The opening services were devotional, with Mrs. Bethune's
contralto voice, deep and rich as a cello, leading the students
in singing, "Leaning On the Everlasting Arms" and in reciting the Twenty-third Psalm. These children had had so
few opportunities that they scarcely knew how to sing to-

gether, but they had come to a woman with a special gift for handling children. She could make a child do anything she wanted him to do.

The parents and other invited guests who crowded into the cottage to watch the ceremony prayed silently for the future of this heroic but impossible dream. Mrs. Bethune stood before them and made as eloquent a speech as though she were starting with several hundred students and addressing a vast audience, seeing beyond them to future Founders' Day ceremonies.

She had far more to do than teach those first students their letters. She mothered them and washed them and taught them manners. If they needed clothing, she begged the material from somewhere and made their dresses and underwear. In Florida at the turn of the century, even after Negroes had been given the rudiments of an education, they could hope only for menial employment. Mrs. Bethune faced facts, and she placed her greatest emphasis on industrial training. She taught her students cooking, housekeeping, and serving, so that they would be equipped to ask for the better-paying domestic jobs.

The lovely little village of Daytona, shaded with giant oaks and pines, soon felt the impact of this new personality. Mary McLeod Bethune talked to everyone who would listen; she spoke in churches whenever she could obtain permission; she went from door to door soliciting donations.

"This is a new kind of school," she explained over and over again. "I am going to teach my girls crafts and home-making. I am going to teach them to earn a living. They will be trained in head, hand, and heart: their heads to think, their hands to work, and their hearts to have faith."

On opening day Mrs. Bethune had possessed not one cent to her name, and so she trained her girls to sing well enough to go around with her to meetings in Daytona and Ormond.

Any heart that had not been softened by Mrs. Bethune's persuasive oratory would be melted by the childish voices raised in unison, and when the heart melted, the pocketbook usually opened.

One day she was scheduled to go with her singing group to the Ormond Hotel on the peninsula, and by that time she had made friends with many of the wealthy white resorters. Henry J. Kaiser carried her group up the Halifax River in his boat so that they would not have to make the long journey around by land. In those days John D. Rockefeller was living at the Ormond Hotel, and he took an immediate fancy to the dark-brown children in blue skirts and white waists singing "Get You Ready" and "Swing Low," and remained a friend of the school until his death.

He loved Negro spiritual music, and after he built his own home on the peninsula, he used to invite Mrs. Bethune to bring her students to sing for him. He usually joined in the singing and beat time. Sometimes the group was ushered into his great circular drawing room where he had white guests, prominent members of the social set, who were all "shushed" to listen to his singers.

Their visits never went unrewarded, because his donations to the school were generous; and every time the children sang they each received a shiny new dime and a slice of cake. The organ in the school was his gift, and long after his death his son John D. Rockefeller, Jr., head of the General Education Board, sent grants of money.

The elder Rockefeller gave Mrs. Bethune his copy of *The Optimist's Good Morning*, compiled by Florence Hobert Perin, a book of wise sayings and comforting thoughts that he had read daily for years.

Mrs. Bethune's school grew faster than her pocketbook in spite of her generous friends. Sometimes her students could afford to pay tuition, and too often they could not. She gathered them all together anyway, determined never to turn away a needy child. On her way home from a round of begging one evening, she came upon two small girls crouched in a doorstep in the darkness, obviously frightened by her approach.

"Where is Mother?"

"She hasn't come home yet."

"Does she go to work?"

"She goes out every day, only today she didn't come home."

"Where's Father?"

"He went away one day when sister was a baby and never came back."

Mrs. Bethune could forget her own needs quickly, and she sat down to talk to the children until their mother finally put in an appearance. She told the mother about her school and asked her to send the girls to her so that they would be cared for during the day. The mother protested that she had no money to pay.

"Don't worry about that," Mrs. Bethune assured her. "Let me take them anyway."

Back in Palatka, Albertus Bethune shook his head as he read letter after letter from his ambitious wife. At first they had been frank about the hardships but full of faith; now they were fraught with excitement and hope. Once more he decided to join her at her new location, and he came to Daytona to move into the second floor of the cottage on Oak Street. He found work driving a taxi—a horse and buggy then—and helped with her school.

Shortly after his arrival, news reached the Bethunes that their cottage on Lemon Street in Palatka had been destroyed by fire, along with everything in it. All of their earthly possessions were gone. Perhaps it was an omen. Perhaps God meant that there should be no turning back.

The first three months flew by, and Christmas was upon them. The Principal of Daytona Industrial and Training School for Negro Girls was making elaborate plans for her students; she wanted this first Christmas to set a precedent for future years. There was to be a program and a fine Christmas dinner. On the morning of the great day the girls bounced around with excitement, practicing their speeches, making every effort to keep themselves spotless, while Mrs. Bethune bustled back and forth, setting the table, overseeing the cooking. Then a knock came at the back door.

A messenger appeared to say that the fashionable lady who had so generously loaned Mrs. Bethune a set of dishes was also giving a large Christmas party. Could she have her dishes back?

There was nothing to do but surrender the only dishes they had; loaned property must be returned. How could there be any Christmas dinner with no dishes? The excitement vanished, the bustling stopped; gloom settled down; the girls began to cry.

"Hush!" said Mrs. Bethune of unshakable faith. "The Lord will provide."

Scarcely had she uttered the sage words when another messenger knocked at the front door. The butler of another resorter stood on the porch, bent over by the weight of a heavy basket.

"Mrs. Lawrence Thompson sent this basket of dishes," he explained. "Her son just gave her a beautiful new set as a Christmas present."

During its first year the school experienced one crisis after another, and oftener than not the problem was food. Mrs. Bethune was close to discouragement one Saturday night when she tried to persuade a grocer to trust her until Monday for four dollars worth of supplies. He refused.

"I'll surely have the money for you on Monday," she

pleaded. "My girls will go hungry if I can't find them something to eat."

The man shook his head firmly, and Mrs. Bethune turned away. Walking slowly home in the gathering dusk, she uttered a prayer with every step she took.

"Dear Lord, please help my children. Help me to provide for them."

As she approached the house she gave a little gasp as she saw sitting on the front steps four big, rough, sinister-looking workmen, obviously from one of the railroad gangs. What had happened? She should never have left the girls unguarded.

"Did you want something?" she asked, trying to keep her voice steady as she approached them.

They stood up respectfully, and each laid a dollar bill in her hand. She had started to teach an adult class in the evenings, and these four men were so grateful that they had decided to pay her.

"Praise the Lord!" cried Mrs. Bethune, and ran back to the grocer.

That was not the only time the cottage had seemed in danger. In addition to the drinking, carousing workmen along the railroad, there was a prison nearby, and occasionally a prisoner escaped.

After the girls were in bed asleep, Mrs. Bethune sat down for a moment of rest. Turning her head to look out of the window, she was startled almost out of her wits to see two men approaching, dressed in prison suits. Hurrying to the door she waited for them.

"Yes?" she demanded.

"Don't be afraid, Ma'am," one said as they mounted the steps. "We're trusties, and we've brought you a present."

They came inside and set down their bundles: fruits and vegetables grown in the prison garden. Mrs. Bethune and her pupils had visited the prison on several Sundays to sing for the men, and they wanted to return her kindness.

In less than two years Mrs. Bethune had two hundred and fifty pupils, and she was using volunteer workers and a few paid teachers. The first teacher, Mrs. Frances Kyles, received the elegant salary of $3.50 a week plus room and board. She was soon followed by Elizabeth Odey, Susie Grant, and others. Desperate for space, Mrs. Bethune rented a building next door and used it for a dormitory and classroom. Every penny she could scrape together went into the school, and she wore old, mended clothes, cutting cardboard soles for her shoes when they wore through.

"I was supposed to keep the balance of the funds for my own pocket, but there never was any balance—only a yawning hole. I wore old clothes sent me by mission boards, recut and redesigned for me in our dressmaking classes. At last I saw that our only solution was to stop renting space and to buy and build our own college."

There was never any lapse of time between the decision and the act where Mrs. Bethune was concerned. She started out at once to hunt for a piece of property, covering Colored Town from one end to the other without any luck. At last she found herself at the western rim of the colored section, looking at the city dump heap, littered with junk, reeking of decaying garbage, swampy and mosquito-infested.

There was a place that no one was using!

She called on the owner at once.

"Why do you want to buy that piece of land?" he asked in amazement. "It's only a public dump heap."

"A dump heap?" said Mrs. Bethune, clasping her hands together and blessing him with one of her winning smiles. "Why, that's not what I see there. I see armies of happy boys and girls going out into life full of hope and faith and knowledge."

He agreed to sell her the land for two hundred dollars; five dollars down and the balance within two years. She hurried away.

"He never knew it, but I didn't have five dollars," she wrote of the transaction. "I promised to be back in a few days with the initial payment. I raised this sum selling ice cream and sweet-potato pies to the workmen on construction jobs, and I took the owner his money in small change wrapped in my handkerchief."

She also took her group of singing girls around to the churches and hotels to perform at fund-raising programs, where she gave speeches to explain the tremendous need for education among the Negroes of the South.

"I had learned already that one of my most important jobs was to be a good beggar! I rang doorbells and tackled cold prospects without a lead. I wrote articles for whoever would print them, distributed leaflets, rode interminable miles of dusty roads on my old bicycle, invaded churches, clubs, lodges, chambers of commerce. If a prospect refused to make a contribution, I would say, 'Thank you for your time.' No matter how deep my hurt, I always smiled. I refused to be discouraged, for neither God nor man can use a discouraged person."

She knew, too, that a school has to be properly organized on a business basis, with a board of trustees to govern it, a board with both Negro and white members.

As she looked through the society columns of a Florida paper, watching for wealthy winter vacationers, she spotted the name of James N. Gamble, of Proctor & Gamble, and promptly wrote him a letter about her school.

"Please call at noon tomorrow," came back his reply.

Borrowing a watch so that she would know the exact time, Mrs. Bethune pedaled her bicycle over to the peninsula. She arrived fifteen minutes early, so she hid behind some shrubbery until the hands of her watch pointed to twelve, then marched up and leaned a strong, work-worn finger on Mr. Gamble's doorbell.

When she was ushered in, the man looked up with frank surprise and said, "Are you the woman trying to build a school here? Why, I thought you were a white woman."

The jet-black Mary Bethune burst out laughing. "Well, you see how white I am."

Without wasting a minute of his time, she told him how desperate the need for such a school was and asked him to be one of its trustees. Mr. Gamble was obviously interested, but he hesitated.

"Why don't you come and visit the school?" she suggested eagerly.

The idea appealed to him, and he agreed to be there the next day. Mrs. Bethune hurried home to a frenzy of scrubbing, sweeping, mending, straightening, to have the cottage in order for the illustrious visitor.

Mr. Gamble was tall and slim, elderly, white-haired, and benign in manner, and he drove up in an antique car chauffeured by another white-haired, benign old gentleman. He looked about him in amazement at the project she had called a "school," staring at the wooden-crate desk, at the students in their altered, mended, and patched dresses.

"And where is this school of which you wish me to be a trustee?" he demanded.

"In my mind, Mr. Gamble!" Mrs. Bethune announced proudly. "And in my soul."

So gracious and kindly a man could not help but admire such courage, and he agreed instantly to become a trustee of the school that existed only in the mind of its creator, handing her a check for one hundred and fifty dollars as a starter.

From then on the industrialist and the educator were partners, and the first project they planned was an inspection day at Oak Street, to which a whole list of prospective trustees and patrons were invited.

The visitors came to the cottage to inspect the dry-goods boxes, charcoal pencils, and handiwork of the students before assembling to watch the exercises. With Mrs. Bethune presiding, the girls who had been running wild only a short time before stood before their visitors to recite and sing, and so impressive was their performance that immediately after the termination of the program the guests elected a chairman, a board of trustees, a secretary and treasurer, and agreed to make their organization permanent.

There is no peace with you,
Nor any rest!
Your presence is a torture to the brain.
Your words are barbed arrows to the breast.

"Enigma" by Jessie Redmond Fauset

9. *Cows, Mules, and Pigs*

To meet her monthly payment on the property, reclaim the land, and erect a new building, Mrs. Bethune's begging efforts had to be doubled and redoubled.

"I hung on to contractors' coattails, begging for loads of sand and secondhand bricks. I went to all the carpenters, mechanics, and plasterers in town, pleading with them to contribute a few hours' work in the evenings in exchange for sandwiches and tuition for their children and themselves."

The new building began to go up slowly, and Mrs. Bethune moved her students in as soon as there was a roof over part of it. Every once in a while the work stopped altogether until more funds could be found.

Mrs. Bethune went from meeting to meeting, speaking

and pleading, taking her pupils with her to sing and recite. She planned what she hoped would be a large gathering of wealthy people at the Palmetto Hotel, one of Daytona's most exclusive resort spots, but because of conflicting social activities only six persons appeared to listen to her. She went ahead with her program anyway, speaking as eloquently to the six as though they were six thousand; and when the collection plate went around, one gentleman dropped in a twenty-dollar bill. It looked like twenty thousand!

She had no idea who her benefactor was, but she was profoundly impressed by his dignified bearing, his gray hair and carefully barbered beard. His kindly gesture was catalogued in the recesses of her memory as she continued her heartbreaking efforts. Once a week she made the rounds of Daytona on her bicycle, stopping at each familiar door, asking for a donation, however small. At the end of the day she would come home with seventy-five or eighty dollars. Many white residents began to look forward to her weekly visit and would have her donation ready for her when she knocked. Some were kind; some were not. Mrs. Steven Bullard, an Australian by birth, was a social leader in Daytona, and an invitation to her teas meant acceptance by everyone else. She was numbered among the less kindly when Mrs. Bethune first began soliciting funds, and could never spare her more than fifty cents. Several years later, on her deathbed, Mrs. Bullard confessed to her friend Mrs. Charles Newbold that she deeply regretted that she had not been more generous to Mrs. Bethune.

One day as Mrs. Bethune cycled along, a huge automobile drew to a stop at her side, and in it sat the bearded gentleman who had given her the twenty dollars.

"Aren't you the one I saw with the children at the Palmetto Hotel?"

Without further conversation, he instructed his chauffeur

to put her bicycle in the back of the car, and together they drove to her new school on Second Avenue.

"I am Thomas H. White of Cleveland," he told her, and she had no idea that he was the manufacturer of the White sewing machines.

He looked around, as every other visitor had done before him, at the unfinished construction, some walls lathed but not plastered, at the homemade mattresses on the beds—for Mrs. Bethune had had to gather Spanish moss from the trees, boil it, dry it, and stuff it into corn sacks for mattresses.

Seeing a box of meal standing in a corner, he asked, "What else is there to eat?"

"That's all we have at the moment," Mrs. Bethune explained.

He heard the familiar whirring sound of a sewing machine and found one of the students struggling with a broken-down Singer.

He turned to Mrs. Bethune abruptly and said, "I believe you are on the right track. This is the most promising thing I've seen in Florida."

He handed her a check for two hundred dollars.

"Oh, two hundred dollars!" Mrs. Bethune's heart sang. "I wept, called the children in for a special meeting. We knelt and thanked God. He came back the next day with a new sewing machine (a White) and with an architect and carpenter, and they brought materials and plaster to put on the walls. And he said, 'I will have bathrooms put in.' He brought pillow slips, sheets."

Time and again he would just drop in with a few pairs of shoes, or blankets, or whatever else seemed necessary. Mrs. Bethune could hardly keep back the tears whenever she talked to him, but he would only reply, "I've never invested a dollar that has brought greater returns than the dollars I've given you."

When he died, he left the school a trust fund of $67,000, the income from which was to be paid "as long as there is a school."

That first building on Second Avenue was of wood, painted white, four stories high, with an open porch across the second-floor level. Over the entrance were emblazoned the words: "Enter To Learn." And over the same door, on the inside: "Depart To Serve."

Faith Hall, named for the Faith Hall of Scotia Seminary, opened officially in 1907; it had been "prayed up, sung up, and talked up," in two years. Yet, opening a building had solved nothing but the space and shelter problems. Clinging to Mrs. Bethune's skirts and hands were two hundred and fifty girls, depending upon her to dress and feed them. They trusted her with the implicit confidence of children; they loved to be gathered in her arms and comforted, to bury their faces in her warm breasts. Children were so helpless; they had to be given everything: knowledge for their minds, love for their hearts, food for their bodies, and warmth during the chill nights of Daytona's winters.

"Let man have dominion over the fish of the sea, and over the fowl of the air, and over the cattle and over all the earth and over every creeping thing that creepeth upon the earth," was all the guidance Mary Bethune needed. She took dominion over her land and made it work for her students. The field across the street from Faith Hall was planted with vegetables, strawberries, flowers, sugar cane. The vegetables, fruits, and flowers were sold to tourists. The girls did their own gardening as part of their regular curriculum; they gathered the cane, crushed it in a cane press, and used the syrup to sweeten their food.

The students had to do everything themselves, because there was only one hired man, Frank Taylor. Devoted but cross, he would watch the vegetables and strawberries with a jealous eye, lest the girls gather the best for themselves. The finest brought higher prices; they must be saved for the tourists. Frank Taylor felt a keen proprietorship in the school; *he* had been with Mrs. Bethune almost from the beginning; *he* had helped pull the moss from the trees, boil it down, dry it, and stuff it into the mattresses for the girls' beds.

A guiding spirit, Frances R. Keyser, joined Mrs. Bethune almost at the beginning. She was quiet, retiring, and soft-spoken, a good balance for Mrs. Bethune. A widow by the time she came to Daytona to teach, she had been the first Negro to graduate from Hunter College in New York City, and, like so many self-sacrificing children of slaves, she had come back to help her people. It was Mrs. Keyser, the school's first dean, who set up the curriculum of study and laid the groundwork for the academic program of the school. Her students dubbed her "the walking encyclopedia," because there seemed to be no end to what she knew. She would take any opportunity to teach. Coming upon a student in the corridor staring up at the reproduction of a painting, she would stop and inquire:

"Do you like that picture?"

A nod.

"It is called 'The Horse Fair,' "—and there would follow the story of the French animal painter, Rosa Bonheur, and an interpretation of her picture.

Enlightened, thrilled, the youngster who had never seen anything more interesting than a farm mule would look again and see the picture transformed into a masterpiece.

Frances Keyser, Portia Smiley, Josie Roberts, and Margaret Seville—Mrs. Bethune called them her "Big Four"—set up the standards of the school in academic, industrial, music, and homemaking work. Mrs. Bethune, with her passionate vigor, furnished the students with their food, shelter, and faith. She was the general who made other people work. Once a visitor found her whitewashing the trees with her right hand while her left hung idle in a sling, because she had pitched down a flight of stairs and broken it. The break had been a particularly painful one that had to be broken and reset. Could others loaf while she carried on in such a manner?

The girls had to have milk; where was it to come from? The farmland needed a mule; where was she to find it? Her talent for persuasive begging produced both; for a tourist visiting Daytona from Ridgewood, New Jersey, agreed that a farm was not a farm without a cow, and donated seventy-five dollars. With gusto, Mary Bethune named the first cow "Ridgewood." A lady from Longmeadow, Massachusetts, donated the second cow, and it was named "Longmeadow."

There wasn't a dime available to buy a mule, but Mrs. Bethune knew where one was for sale. With a tourist in tow, she opened the conversation cautiously:

"Are you a good judge of mules?"

"Pretty fair."

"There's one for sale that I want to buy, but I'm not sure whether the animal is worth what the man is asking. Would you be kind enough to go and look at it for me and let me know what you think?"

If the visitor knew that Mrs. Bethune had grown up on a South Carolina farm where the mule was almost a member of the family, he did not let on. He promised to look at the animal, and a few days later he came back and said:

"I saw the mule. He is a little old, but I think he is pretty good."

Then he went away.

"I got weak in the knees," wrote Mrs. Bethune. "I followed him to the gate, but he said nothing more about the mule. I came back to my desk and went to work, holding the thought that he would get it. Night came; I went to bed and dreamed about that mule. Early in the morning a telephone message came: 'Mrs. Bethune, I told that man to send the mule out there, and if you haven't the money to pay for it, go to the post office. You will find a check there.' "

In 1908 Mrs. Bethune changed the name of her school to Daytona Educational Industrial Training School, and a few boys were taken as students.

That same year saw, in the midst of all its strain and worry, the excitement of another great Negro personality, when Booker T. Washington visited the school, bringing encouragement and inspiration with him.

Born a slave, Booker T. Washington had no exact record of his birth, but he was about fifty when he visited Daytona. *Up From Slavery* he had called the story of his own life, because as a child he had prayed with his elders for victory for the Northern armies, had lived through the struggle for an education, devouring any printed matter he could get his hands on, hitchhiking from one state to another in search of a school that would admit him, working his way through Hampton Institute in Virginia. Like Mrs. Bethune, he had remained in the South, going to Alabama in response to an appeal for a teacher from Negro leaders of Tuskegee town to found Tuskegee Institute in the midst of the most deplorable conditions.

By the time he visited Mrs. Bethune's school, Tuskegee Institute, which had begun with a shanty and a hen house, one teacher and thirty students, had more than sixty buildings, hundreds of acres of land, and strong financial support.

As he strolled about, looking at the Daytona Institute grounds and building, the gardens and livestock, which by now included pigs, he shook his head, realizing how much discouragement was still in the immediate future, having lived through the same thing himself.

"I don't see how you will ever bridge the chasm between

the needs of the school and what you have," he said. "But I'm sure you will, somehow."

There weren't sufficient facilities to accommodate him and his dozen associates, but Mrs. Bethune's ingenuity and the generosity of her white and Negro friends filled the breach quickly. She gave Dr. Washington her own room. Neighbors brought linens and blankets and extra food. Messrs. White and Gamble loaned their automobiles. The guests ate baked beans for breakfast, and Mrs. Bethune gathered wild violets for Dr. Washington's lapel.

During his stay, Dr. Washington spoke at a public meeting held in the armory building in Daytona. Hundreds, both black and white, packed the hall and packed the streets around the hall to hear him, for he had bridged the gap between the races in a way that even the most bigoted white had to acknowledge was constructive. He asked both whites and Negroes to be patient with one another.

He was well informed on the details of Negro life in every state in the Union; in addition to his teaching, administration, and fund raising at Tuskegee, he subscribed to a press-clipping service and kept up a tremendous volume of correspondence. He encouraged people to write to him, and he answered mail promptly. He watched for Negro achievements and wrote letters of congratulation, even if it was only the winning of a prize at a county fair in some out-of-the-way community.

"Some day we will have more Negro doctors, lawyers, statesmen, scientists, as well as more artisans and better farmers," Mrs. Bethune and Dr. Washington dreamed together. "Some day the Negro will be allowed to live in peace and safety, in dignity and culture. He will be allowed to attend the best universities—"

They stopped before the pigpen where two fat. honking

animals were pushing their disk snouts through the mud, and Dr. Washington nodded his approval.

"I'm glad you have pigs," he said. "They are my favorite farm animal. The pig is a mortgage lifter. Once at a farm conference at Tuskegee a woman got up and said, 'Mr. Washington, yo' is got befo' yo' now Sister Nelson of Tallapoosa County, Alabama. All I has I owes to dis conference and one little puppy dog. I got a little pig from dat little puppy dog an' I got my prosperity from dat pig!' She had exchanged the puppy for a pig, bred the pig again and again, selling the litters to neighbors. With the proceeds she bought a cow and began selling milk. Then she bought land for a garden and is selling the vegetables, too."

Mrs. Bethune stored the advice away in her heart. Each night, after her conferences with Booker T. Washington, the ardent young woman, still only thirty-three, would bury her face in her hands and pray, "Dear Lord, help my people! Help me to help my people!"

After he and his party said farewell, she returned to her work with even more vigor than before. She had been blessed by the approval of a man who had met and overcome conditions such as she was facing.

Shortly after Dr. Washington's departure, Mary Bethune dreamed her third great dream. In it, she thought she was sitting on the bank of the Halifax River, and she was gazing into the water, wondering how she would ever build her school. The sound of galloping hoofs startled her out of her reverie, and she turned her head toward the sound. Down Beach Street sped a handsome saddle horse, the rider all in uniform, with a huge hat on his head. He pulled the horse to a stop in front of her, dismounted, and threw the reins over a stake.

"What are you doing here?" he inquired.

"Who are you?" she asked, perplexed.

"I am Booker T. Washington."

"Oh, Mr. Washington, I am just sitting here trying to think of some plan, some way by which I can build my school."

He thrust his hand into his hip pocket and pulled out a soiled handkerchief, and out of the center of the crumbled handkerchief he drew a huge, glittering diamond. Handing the precious gem to Mary Bethune, he said,

"Take this and build your school."

With that he turned to his horse, mounted, and galloped off.

She awoke with a start. The dream had seemed so real that she looked in her hand for the diamond. He *had* given her a diamond, a gem of greater price than the human heart could measure.

I thought I saw an angel flying low,
I thought I saw the flicker of a wing.

"Nocturne at Bethesda" by Arna Bontemps

10. *Mercy Spot*

Life at Mrs. Bethune's school was never to be easy. There would always be a gnawing worry over money, for as soon as funds came in, they were swallowed up by unpaid teachers' salaries, grocery bills, repairs, supplies; and the creditors who were still unsatisfied would ask bluntly, "When do you expect some more money?"

She always replied calmly, "You know we always pay; you will get your money soon."

But progress was ever forward. The school gardens flourished, and tourists learned that they could buy finer vegetables on Second Avenue than elsewhere in town. A large display stand made its appearance beside the road, and wealthy white folk ventured across the tracks and along the muddy, unpaved street for corn, string beans, carrots, bunches of sweet peas; and the pennies and nickels dribbled in to the yawning school treasury.

The number of students increased as Mrs. Keyser traveled around the State of Florida between school terms to recruit new children, persuading their parents to allow them to live at the school for a term or a year, then returning to persuade them to leave the youngsters longer. The tuition was kept low, but sometimes the child who most needed the school could least afford to pay. Mrs. Keyser and Mrs. Bethune saw to it that the money came from somewhere, somehow.

The scholastic level of the school grew higher and higher, for the five original students who had started as first graders were sixth graders in 1910. Older children had come in later and were still further along. It was Mrs. Bethune's purpose to promote her students so that each class completed formed the next higher grade, until it was possible to have a graduating class from the eighth grade. Soon she was able to give work at a high-school level.

To one of those very early graduation days came a workworn, aging widow who had once been a slave—Patsy McLeod—to pay a visit to this fabulous daughter of hers. She arrived in Daytona a little unnerved from her first train ride, dressed in her best black alpaca and with a little lace cap over her white hair. When she saw the handsome young woman, whose figure had grown buxom and matronly, come toward her, she held out her arms.

"Janie! Janie!"

Mrs. Bethune laughed and cried with her; she had almost forgotten she had once been Janie, since so many children now turned to her as a mother.

"Mama, wait until you see my school. Wait until you see! I have nearly four hundred children; we're crowded but we're happy."

Once again on graduation day Patsy McLeod listened

to essays of students, speeches by important civic leaders, both Negro and white, and saw rolls of diplomas being handed out. The hand that presented them had once reached up eagerly to grasp her own, holding lovingly that precious insurance against the mocking words, "Put down that book! *You* can't read!"

Mary McLeod Bethune wanted to reach everyone; so she planned evening classes for adult Negroes, to lift them out of their dismal illiteracy and teach them to live more wholesomely. She invaded their drab cabins, taught them to paint the walls, put curtains on the windows, rugs on the floors. As soon as the parents of her students were persuaded to come to school to learn their letters, she added the rudiments of art and music to their curriculum. Upon being shown how to draw, one elderly lady said, "I never knew that you could make flowers like that on paper."

She was left to handle alone her monumental task and the raising of her son shortly after moving into Faith Hall, when her husband obtained a teaching post in a nearby city. A man with his education was, of course, not satisfied with the employment he had been able to obtain in Daytona; and it seemed wise for him to accept the new position, even though it meant that the family would be separated.

Albert, Junior, remained with his mother and attended classes at her school until he was old enough for a man's institute. Frequently she took him with her when she went about town shopping or soliciting funds for her school, and he was sensitive enough to wonder about the strangely divided world in which they lived.

"You must pull your hat to all the ladies you meet," his mother had explained to him. "Always pull your cap to the ladies."

As mother and son walked down Second Avenue, a white lady passed them in the other direction, nodding and smiling to the couple. Mrs. Bethune nodded and smiled as she always did, and her son pulled his cap.

In the next block a small white boy of Albert's age passed them.

"How do you do, little boy," said the woman who was a friend of all children.

The youngster looked at them and went on without speaking or tipping his hat.

"Mother, why didn't the white boy tip his hat to you?" came the inevitable question.

"I don't know what that boy's mother wants him to be," she replied quickly. "But I want you to be a gentleman. We must have love in our hearts, not hate."

She knew she could not protect her son forever from knowing the world in which he would have to live, and she knew she could not solve race prejudice singlehanded. She did what she could to arm him and her other students with faith and wholesome thinking, and she fought every waking minute against bigotry. To every white person she gave a gracious smile and accepted either a smile or rebuff in exchange. Some, she knew, would never give an inch. One man whom she always greeted pleasantly always repaid her with silence, and when she persisted with her cheerful "good morning" he stopped and confronted her.

"Why do you speak to me? Can't you see I don't want anything to do with you? Why don't you let me alone? I don't want your good morning."

Mrs. Bethune begged his pardon.

The Daytona Educational Industrial Training School was more than a school; it was a light in the midst of darkness; it was a great social mission from which workers went out in every direction into the shadowy byways of vice and destitution.

When Mrs. Bethune first took up residence in Daytona,

she had heard rumors of conditions in the turpentine camps, and she stored the information in the back of her memory. By 1911 she had students who were old enough and sufficiently trained to help her tackle the problem.

Turpentine is made from the sap of the slash pine, and Florida, especially in the northern half of the state, has miles and miles of such pine forests. Trees are tapped by cutting away the bark in V-shaped ridges and putting an earthenware cup at the bottom of the cut to catch the gummy sap or pitch. The pitch is gathered and distilled into turpentine and resin.

A manufacturer would buy a large tract of pine forest, build a few shanties and distilleries, then round up the ne'erdo-wells and riffraff in the area, pay them low wages, guarantee them all the rum they could drink, and set them to work gathering turpentine. Drunkenness, ribaldry, immorality, and sickness were rampant, and what women and children were with the men soon succumbed to the conditions. The expression "turpentine camp" was enough to send a shudder down the backs of the respectable.

Gathering a group of her older students together one Sunday afternoon, Mrs. Bethune started for a turpentine camp only three miles from Daytona. When they reached the camp and saw the impossible task they must tackle, her protégées held back.

"Don't be afraid," she said firmly. "Have faith."

The first shanty they saw was obviously the source of the rum. Negroes sprawled on the ground nearby. One, barely able to remain on his feet, lurched toward the visiting party with a raucous laugh. Mrs. Bethune brushed past him when she saw a ragged, unkempt woman hiding timidly behind a tree. Cadaverous cheeks and glassy eyes suggested malnutrition, possibly tuberculosis. Mrs. Bethune approached her and held out a hand of mercy.

"Better not stay," was the advice. "Better not stay."

She had heard that kind of advice before. "Better not stay in Daytona," she had been told. "You just don't realize how bad conditions are here."

"Where are the children? Who is caring for them?" she demanded.

The woman made a hopeless gesture with her hand toward the forest.

"All about," she answered in a dead, flat voice.

Mrs. Bethune and her disciples found one shanty that would serve as a church, and she gathered into a meeting as many as would come. They laughed, they jeered, they invented vulgar jokes; some even brought their rum bottles, lest thirst overtake them during the meeting.

Patiently, gently, Mary McLeod Bethune sang the first note of a hymn in her unforgettable rich contralto, and her students joined their voices with hers. As the music grew into a crescendo, the jeering and laughter died down; rum bottles were eased quietly to the floor. She finished the hymn and sang another. With their attention secured, Mrs. Bethune spoke to them in simple, eloquent words about the evil of their lives. She planned to come back every Sunday afternoon to read and sing to them, she promised, and some day she would open a school, which she hoped every child in the camp would attend.

Eventually she was able to start the school and the children did come, eagerly learning to sing, to sew, to play organized games, to read and write. Once she had made contact with the children, she went into their homes to teach the parents cleanliness, wholesome cooking, sober living.

One mother commented timidly, "We do hope that you will keep on coming, because we sure appreciate your visits to our homes and your work with our children."

Hearing about another turpentine camp two miles beyond,

Mrs. Bethune left her trainees in charge of the first mission and pushed on to establish a second; and after the second, a third and fourth.

Within five years she had a chain of mission schools, the Tomoka Missions, operating throughout the turpentine camps, staffed by her own students. The children in the camps were receiving three months' schooling every year; the workmen were getting higher wages, doing considerably less drinking or none at all, and saving their surplus money.

The smallest episode or an isolated incident could fire Mrs. Bethune's imagination with an idea for a whole new civic program.

She was called hurriedly to the bedside of a student, to find the youngster doubled up with abdominal pain and running a high temperature. She did not have to be a doctor to see that the sufferer was stricken with acute appendicitis and must have an operation immediately. Thereby hung another tragedy. No hospitals for Negroes!

"I went to a local hospital and begged a white physician to take her in and operate," she related. "My pleas were so desperate he finally agreed."

In a day or two Mrs. Bethune reappeared at the door of the hospital and asked to see her pupil. The nurse ordered her around to the back door. Sometimes Mrs. Bethune complied with the white man's wishes and sometimes she did not; this day she brushed the nurse aside and marched in. After a short search she found her girl segregated on a porch behind the kitchen, subject to the commotion and smells of the endless preparation of food.

"Even my toes clenched with rage!" was her description of her anger as she stood helplessly looking down at the neglected, ill-cared-for patient.

Others might submit meekly to this injustice, but she did not intend to; Daytona Negroes must have a hospital. So she hurried back to her office and began writing letters to her most faithful supporters. There was a frame cottage on the street in back of Faith Hall, she explained, that would make an excellent hospital building, total cost to be about five thousand dollars. Would they please help her buy it? The funds began to come in, and when she had raised about four thousand dollars, Andrew Carnegie sent her the last thousand.

She had been able to "pray up, sing up, and talk up" Faith Hall and keep it in operation; in the same way she was able to "pray up, sing up, and talk up" McLeod Hospital, and it became a source of mercy for the entire east coast. Starting with two beds in 1911, in a few years she had a well-equipped, twenty-bed hospital, with both Negro and white physicians and her own student nurses. Her school operated the hospital for twenty years, until Daytona finally consented to provide a hospital for Negroes on the same grounds as the city hospital.

Time and again during those twenty years the white world was forced to turn to McLeod Hospital for help. An explosion in a nearby rockworks brought the owner to the campus of Daytona Educational Industrial Training School looking for "Mary," because some of his "niggers" had been hurt in the accident. With a prayer on her lips: "Lord, make me give him the answer that will do the most good," Mrs. Bethune put in an appearance. His vocabulary wasn't new to her; she had been hearing it all her life, and she had extraordinary finesse in handling rude white men.

"I'm *Mrs.* Bethune. Are you looking for me?"

"Some of my 'nig—', I mean, colored workmen were hurt in a blast at the rockworks, and I want to bring them to your hospital."

"Very well, we can take care of them."

"Now, don't baby them. They are workers."

"We have doctors here who determine how sick a man is and how much care he will need."

Taken aback by her gentle voice and complete lack of fear, he asked with considerably less arrogance, "How much do you want?"

"You will have to ask the man in charge. We have a system here, just as I assume you have at your rockworks."

The man shrunk deeper into his collar and said, "Thank you, *Mrs.* Bethune."

McLeod Hospital extended its helping hand again during the influenza epidemic of 1918, when the prompt and efficient work of Mrs. Bethune's staff of nurses received public acclaim. The hospital was filled to overflowing, and rows of cots had to be placed in the school auditorium.

A year after she had started the first turpentine mission, and four years after Booker T. Washington's visit to her school, Mrs. Bethune attended a conference at Tuskegee Institute in Alabama. Through this renewed association with Dr. Washington she caught another vision: the community conference.

When Dr. Washington first went into Alabama to found Tuskegee, he had to teach his people everything from brushing their teeth to running their farms, and he depended heavily on having one teach another. So, early in the life of his school, he started holding annual experience meetings, the Tuskegee Negro Conferences. To them came farmers from far and wide to give testimony to their progress, thanks to help received from their adored and venerated Dr. Washington and his associates. It was at one of these conferences that the woman had told the story of the puppy and the pig. Another tall, handsome man stood up in a meeting and reported that he had changed from being worth nothing to owning his own home, two hundred acres of land, both free of debt, and

two bank accounts—all the result of Dr. Washington's conferences.

Intensive research in agriculture was conducted at Tuskegee all the time, and as fast as new knowledge was discovered,
it was passed on to all who could be persuaded to accept it.
Dr. Washington even founded a weekly farm journal to
spread his teachings.

Mary McLeod Bethune, until now more or less cut off from
the rest of the world because of the demands made upon her
by her own school, thought she would not be able to stand
the excitement of hearing of the progress of Negroes all over
the United States. Emancipation had occurred only half a
century before, yet as a result of the tremendous efforts of
their own leaders, Negroes could boast of owning their own
farms, of being able to read and write, of operating Negro
banks, drugstores, retail shops, and wholesale establishments.

She witnessed the mass meetings that sat spellbound listening to Dr. Washington's eloquence as he praised, cajoled,
scolded, taught, and inspired. She strolled about the campus,
looking at the buildings constructed by the students out of
their own handmade bricks, and she consulted with other
members of the Tuskegee staff. She met Dr. George Washington Carver at that conference, too, and promptly acquired
another hero.

The slightly built, humble, sweet-dispositioned scientist
had been at Tuskegee since 1896, when he had joined the
staff to take charge of the Agriculture Department. Dr. Carver
investigated every weed that grew by the roadside for its edi-
bility or medicinal value. When he saw a pumpkin plant
growing lustily in a garbage heap, he hit upon the idea of
using organic waste for fertilizer. He took the unknown and
unnoticed soybean into his laboratory and discovered its high
food value. Looking at the soil of the South made barren by

years of planting nothing but cotton, he realized that the South needed new crops and rotation of crops. One of the most widely known of Dr. Carver's new crops was the peanut plant. He found that the peanut contains more protein than sirloin steak, more carbohydrates than potatoes, better fat than butter. In order to create a demand for the new crop so that farmers would plant it, he worked night and day to develop dishes made from peanuts and to discover new peanut products. He gave a luncheon to key people, serving soup, mock chicken, salad, bread, candy, cake, ice cream, and coffee, each course made entirely of peanuts. He discovered that from peanuts one could make washing powder, metal polish, paper, ink, shaving cream, axle grease, sauces, beverages. Out of his humble laboratory and fifteen-hundred-dollar-a-year salary, a whole new industry was born, one that would rescue the cotton growers from their poverty—and never a copyright to protect any of it, because Dr. Carver never cared about money. He wanted his discoveries to be shared by all. Born in slavery and poverty himself, doing the most menial work to earn his way through school, he emerged as a kind of scientific Moses to his people.

Mrs. Bethune spent many pleasant hours with him, and he became fond of her and liked to take her around his laboratory and study, telling her of things he had done and that he anticipated doing.

"I had a great admiration for him," she said later. "I think he is one of the most unusual people I have ever met."

When one of the men on the campus wanted to take their picture together, Mrs. Bethune protested because she knew Dr. Carver was in bed with a cold. But Dr. Carver arose and dressed, appearing in a red necktie and commenting to Mrs. Bethune, "Sweetheart, I wouldn't have dressed myself and come out for anyone else but you."

Together, Dr. Carver and Mrs. Bethune received honorary degrees of Doctor of Science from Tuskegee Institute.

Refreshed, thrilled, inspired to even greater efforts, Mrs. Bethune returned to Daytona and looked about her.

"We need a community conference," she announced in her powerful voice; and *her* staff knew that when she assumed that tone a community conference would surely take place.

She planned, organized, and brought into being a conference and baby show for all of Volusia County, the county in which Daytona is located. Prizes were given for the finest vegetables, jellies, and needlework. The women proudly presented their babies to show how well cared-for they were, or they met together to exchange ideas and listen to advice on baby care. Mrs. Bethune also offered a prize of a new rake and hoe for the best-kept cabin and yard, and that gave her the excuse she needed, before the conference, to drive around the county on inspection tours, viewing litter with a fierce eye.

"Maybe I won't get the prize," one man commented. "But I sure ain't going to let that committee come around here and find a lot of old tin cans and all sorts of rubbish in my back yard. No, sir!"

His companion looked up with alarm and asked, "You don't reckon they're going into the back yard?"

"Hush, man! Don't you know who's head of this thing? You know Mrs. Bethune, and she's going into the back yard. You know we call her the 'dirt chaser,' so you better clean up your little place, too."

The Negroes derived so much instruction in better living from that first conference that the idea soon spread to three counties. The competitive spirit of the conferences made them want more attractive homes, better gardens, healthier children.

Thy various works, imperial queen, we see,
How bright their forms! how deck'd with
pomp by thee!

"On Imagination" by Phillis Wheatley

II. *Any Sunday Afternoon*

Mary Bethune's biggest effort was always for her school. No matter how many other responsibilities she assumed, her charges came first, because she knew that the young people she was training would go out in every direction and carry on long after her own life's work was done.

By 1914 Daytona Educational Industrial Training School was offering a full high-school course and turning out graduates every spring in homemaking, teaching, cooking, and nursing. As its founder walked through the corridors of Faith Hall and looked into one crowded classroom after another, she remembered the hovel on Oak Street, furnished with battered relics from the public dump heaps, and her roll of five girls.

Or she went into the school kitchen where the motto on the wall said: "Cease to be a drudge; seek to be an artist," and watched the girls learning to prepare tasty dishes and balanced meals. From Faith Hall she walked across the school grounds and glanced over the additional acres of swamp she had been able to acquire and reclaim, now gardens and grazing land. In McLeod Hospital patients lay comfortably in clean beds attended by her own student nurses.

She had cracked her whip over a lot of heads to achieve all this. Careless or untidy hearts sank when she came by on inspection, because they knew how she felt about indifferent effort, mussed rooms, or unwashed hands.

Each student gave an hour a day to the care of the school, keeping the place spic and span from attic to basement, and had an opportunity to work at every kind of household task, so that tasks were also training: bathroom, hall, steps, the kitchen. Every girl had to learn to bake bread, for instance, and was assigned this responsibility for three weeks. New girls came in for bread baking every two weeks, so the outgoing students could teach the new ones the system. They set up the dough the night before and worked at it all the next day, baking twice a week. Each teacher had a girl assigned to take care of her room.

Mrs. Bethune would go into a student's room and turn back the bed cover to see if the sheets were clean and smooth. She would inspect trunks and closets—even persons. A sponge bath every day with the wash bowl and pitcher in the room, and a tub bath every Wednesday and Saturday night of your life! Supervised and checked! On Wednesday night, clean clothing from the skin out had to be placed neatly on the chair beside the bed. There was a pail for refuse in every room that must be taken out and scrubbed. Each bucket had a number and a hook, and it was inspected in the morning. If a bucket was missing, it had to be accounted for.

Tourists could come to the campus and test the dusting with their white gloves; they were encouraged to look at cupboard shelves, clothes closets, desk drawers. Oftener than not, the cleanliness and good management of the place won an extra donation.

Hand in hand with cleanliness went thrift.

"Thrift," Mrs. Bethune always said, "is doing something and having something to show for it."

Plant strawberries in the school garden, was what she meant, only don't eat them yourself. Sell them to the tourists and use the proceeds to buy meat for the student body.

Even the moss-hung, evergreen oaks that had provided stuffing for the first mattresses were still exploited in the name of thrift. They yielded acorns that fed the pigs, and every spring the girls were organized into pig clubs, crews of eight or ten, to gather the acorns and rake the lawns. Not an acorn lay on the ground when they had finished their job.

When all the economies had been attended to, all the lessons completed, and all the chores checked off, singing was the pastime the students enjoyed most, sharing it with each other and with the community of Daytona. They loved to sing during their own chapel services. At Christmas time they went about town singing Christmas carols, especially on the peninsula side where the wealthy white homes were located. Often, word would be sent to the school that Mrs. So-and-so was having guests on Christmas Eve, and would the carolers please be sure to stop outside her home? Frequently the dark-brown angels of the glad tidings would be invited in and treated to cake, or Mrs. Bethune would be given a donation for her school.

The idea of singing groups had come from Fisk University in Nashville, Tennessee. Fisk Jubilee Singers were the first group to gather together and arrange artistically the wealth of unrecorded Negro folk songs. Traveling about the country and abroad, these young Negro singers appeared before large audiences, and their popularity grew with the rising appreciation for their music. Their purpose was to raise money for Fisk, and they were so successful that other Negro schools copied the idea.

Mrs. Bethune went on excursions into the North with a group of singing girls, and she found they had a profoundly lucrative and sentimental appeal for white people.

On one of her trips North, she stopped off in Washington to look up an old friend, "Teets" Cantey, Mrs. Cecelia Smith by that time.

The onetime young charge of Scotia threw her arms around the visitor in joy, stood back and held her at arms' length, and began to scold.

"Look at you!"

"You're looking at me, Teets. What's wrong?"

"Your clothes! They're awful, all out of date and frayed. You can't go to New York looking like that."

"I don't care about my clothes. They're clean. That's sufficient."

"Humph!"

After dinner, Teets Cantey Smith dug into her closets and cupboards and came out with clothing.

"Are those for my children?" asked Mary Bethune eagerly.

"No! These are for *you*. Now, give me that coat you are wearing, so that I can sew this fur on the collar and cuffs. And here is a whole pair of stockings."

The little girl who had once sat on Mrs. Bethune's lap now took charge of her protector and sent her forth looking much more prosperous and stylish.

Mrs. Bethune traveled around raising funds, watched over her community in Daytona like a mother hen, and kept up a volume of correspondence with friends and associates all over the United States. Her influence was increasing day by day.

Probably the only cloud on her horizon in those days was the news of her mother's death in 1915, when the aged lady, the onetime slave, at last relinquished her last breath to the pressure of years. Her father had died nine years earlier in 1906.

The daughter of the slave pushed onward and upward with her boundless energy, and students crowded into her school until it virtually began to burst at the seams.

Everything she did was still based on faith. When others around her shook their heads and uttered the word "impossible," Mrs. Bethune, the stubborn woman with the strong, protruding jaw, would say, "Go ahead and do it."

One of the buildings needed a new roof, and there were no funds available for the extra expense. Mrs. Bethune had tried everywhere to raise the money, with no success whatsoever. Having waited as long as her patience would allow, she walked out onto the campus, called the carpenters together, and said, "We have enough old lumber lying around. Put up the scaffolds."

"Mrs. Bethune," they protested, "what's the use? What good is the scaffolding if you can't buy the shingles or pay the roofers?"

"Put up the scaffolding! God will provide."

They obeyed with much grumbling and scowling at Mrs. Bethune's back as she walked to her office, where she sat down and began to open her mail. Bills, bills, bills! One after another she read messages from creditors who wanted to know when they could expect something on account. At the bottom of the pile was a letter bearing a Tarrytown, New York, postmark. At least this would not be a bill. Much better, it was a note of encouragement from an admirer who enclosed a check for $1000.

Faith Hall had become much too small and inadequate for its tasks. One frame building could no longer be residence hall, school, kitchen, laundry, and chapel. Mrs. Bethune began to extend her dreaming again. A new building? Ah, yes! It would be of brick this time, not a perishable wooden frame structure succumbing slowly but surely to the humid, semitropical climate and termites of Florida. It would be large, much larger than Faith Hall, with modern conveniences, plumbing, electric lights, offices for principal and dean, classrooms for the bulging enrollment, and a chapel for worship. It would stand on the west side of Faith Hall, and she would transfer the mottoes from Faith Hall to the new building. Outside the main entrance would be blazoned the words: "Enter To Learn." Inside, to counsel those leaving the school, would be the words, "Depart To Serve."

The money for this edifice? She had raised money for Faith Hall and for the hospital; she could, with God's help, raise more. She would go to her wealthy white friends and explain this newest dream, this tremendous need.

"Please, dear Lord," she began to pray. "Give me the power to convince these people that I need the money."

God gave her such powers of persuasion that she needed to talk to only two persons: Thomas H. White and James N. Gamble. They provided the entire amount. Within a few months Mrs. Bethune could stand out on Second Avenue, hands on hips, and watch the gathering stack of bricks, piles of sand, loads of lumber, bags of cement.

"What are you going to call this building?" she was asked.

"White Hall, of course," she responded quickly.

How could anyone have thought she would do otherwise?

The dedication of White Hall in 1916 was a rare contrast to the pathetic scene that had taken place in 1904 with five little girls in the cottage on Oak Street. A long procession of students, teachers, advisers, and the Board of Trustees marched along the campus and filed solemnly up the front steps through the white-columned entrance and the corridor to the chapel, large enough to seat six hundred. Thomas R. Marshall, Vice President of the United States, and Sydney J. Catts, the Governor of Florida, gave addresses; so did Emmett J. Scott, formerly secretary to Dr. Booker T. Washington, and at that time secretary-treasurer of Howard University in Washington, D. C.

When the keys of the new building were presented to Mrs. Bethune, she reached out trembling hands to receive them—humble, work-worn hands that were extended to accept whatever help the world was willing to drop into them. Mary McLeod Bethune stood on the platform facing her student body, and she turned and handed the keys to James N. Gamble, still president of the Board of Trustees. Another dream had become a fact!

Like all of her projects, this new building was destined to serve the entire community. Every Sunday afternoon the residents of Daytona came to the college chapel for a worship service.

Patterning the meetings along the lines of those held at Lucy Laney's school in Augusta, Mrs. Bethune, shortly after opening Faith Hall, had started holding interracial services at three o'clock every Sunday. The students sang hymns, recited poems both classical and original; Mrs. Bethune or another faculty member gave a short sermon and led in prayer. Spontaneous and unplanned, the spiritual vitality of the meetings attracted larger and larger crowds from both sides of the Halifax River, until latecomers had to stand outside on the porch.

The new chapel meant that the Sunday afternoon services could be expanded and all guests accommodated.

The meetings are still popular in Daytona. Any Sunday afternoon will see resorters strolling or driving across the bridge that spans the river, and across the railroad tracks, to Second Avenue for fraternal worship. Through its Sunday af-

1. *The cabin in which Mary McLeod was born*

2. *A five-mile walk along this road every day to school*

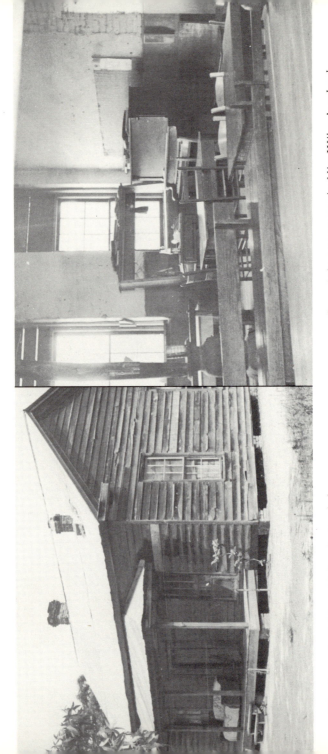

4. *One of the two rooms in Miss Wilson's school*

3. *The first school Mary McLeod attended*

5. *Mary McLeod when she graduated from Moody Bible Institute*

6. *The original Faith Hall in Daytona Beach*

7. *Students and faculty grinding their own sugar cane
at Daytona Industrial School in the early days*

8. *Raising their own vegetables
across the street from the school in Daytona*

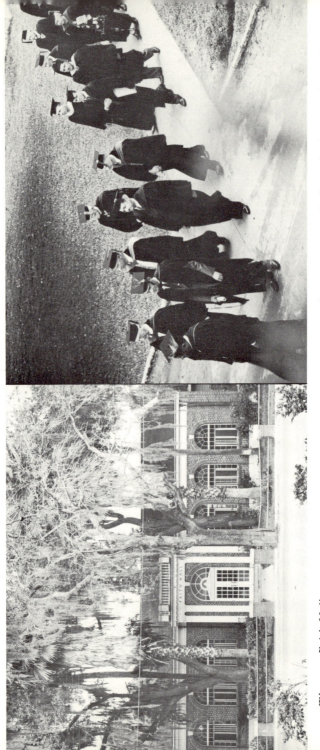

10.   *Campus scene at Bethune-Cookman College today*

9.   *The new Faith Hall*

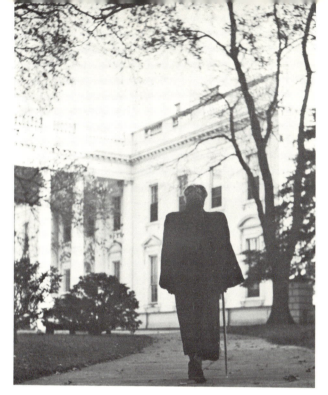

11. *President Roosevelt depended upon her*

12. *Mrs. Roosevelt calling on Mrs. Bethune in her office*

13. *Mrs. Bethune with Olveta Culp Hobby*

14. *Mrs. Bethune at seventy-five*

ternoon meetings, Bethune-Cookman College has become one of the greatest interracial laboratories in the entire South. People of all races, creeds, and colors sit side by side.

"Why, I haven't missed one of those services in years," a winter vacationer is heard to comment. "I love the enthusiasm of those young people."

Bewildered we are, and passion-tost, mad with the madness of a mobbed and mocked and murdered people.

"A Litany at Atlanta" by William Edward Burghardt DuBois

12. *The Ku Klux Klan*

The mingling of races in the chapel at Daytona Educational Industrial Training School was a small part of a greater movement toward understanding that was taking place all over the United States. At the turn of the century America was discovering the Negro, his folk tales and legends, his work songs and spirituals. The fox trot, ragtime, "blues" music, the Charleston, jazz all grew out of Negro rhythms and folk songs. The Negro has contributed as much to American culture as the Pilgrims, the Spanish explorers, the French settlers, and all the other types who melted together to create a new nation.

But the picture of the Negro's contributions has been clouded by hatred and crime. During the first decade of the twentieth century terrible race riots occurred. One of the worst took place in Statesboro, Georgia, in 1904. Two Negroes were arrested and charged with the murder of a white farmer and his family. They were tried in Savannah, and of course they were convicted and sentenced to be hanged, because a Negro's testimony was not acceptable in a white man's court. Outside the jail, hysteria began to mount. The Negroes were getting out of hand! They were murderers, attackers of white women! Fantastic stories were told and retold by careless newspapers. Out of the craze a lynch mob developed which stormed the jail, beat back the Savannah militia, dragged the two Negroes out and burned them alive. This accomplished, the mob turned on any unfortunate Negro within its reach; whippings, looting, arson followed. The fury did not spend itself for several days.

Two years later, a major race riot occurred in Atlanta, Georgia; and another in Brownsville, Texas, in the same year. The poison spread to the North, and Springfield, Illinois, experienced one of the worst race riots that have ever occurred. It all began on a false charge: a white woman accused a Negro of dragging her out of her house and assaulting her. Even though she changed her testimony and admitted that her assailant had been a white man, public feeling against the Negro began to mount. Soon frenzied mobs were milling through the streets, ready to set hands on any Negro. A barber was lynched for no reason at all, and his body dragged through the streets as an example to others.

Before 1900, thousands of lynchings occurred in all parts of the United States except New England. Mississippi had the most, with Georgia a close second. After 1900 the number began to decrease, and each year there were fewer lynchings, until in 1950 there were only two.

When Negro leaders met in conference to discuss their problems, the reason for the decreased number of lynchings and riots and for the increased racial understanding became evident. The Negro's educational level was rising, and with it his resistance to violence and his insistence on the protection afforded by the law. By 1900 a million and a half Negro children were in school, with nearly thirty thousand Negro teachers instructing them, and there were thirty-four Negro colleges and universities.

Negroes' progress in obtaining civil rights was helped still further when Theodore Roosevelt became President in that year. He took a vigorous personal interest in their welfare, encouraged them to greater effort, became a close friend of Booker T. Washington, and even visited Tuskegee. During his two terms in office, Americans of Negro descent began once more to experience real progress along the road to equality.

From the turn of the eighteenth century through the period of the Civil War and Reconstruction, American Negroes had had so many special problems to solve—illiteracy, segregation, low wages and living standards, lynchings—that relatively few of them had developed any interest in the rest of the world. The news that a British ship, the *Lusitania*, had been torpedoed by a German submarine and sunk with great loss of life had little meaning for the mass of Negroes, especially in the backward areas of the South. When Woodrow Wilson was re-elected to the Presidency in November, 1916, many did not realize that the great Democrat was unsympathetic, even intolerant, toward Negroes, and that under his first administration Negroes had not fared at all well. The number of Negroes in federal employment had decreased, and Jim Crow regulations in washrooms, restaurants, and offices had become more stringent. In the Navy Department, screens were set up, separating white and Negro workers.

When the United States declared war on Germany in 1917, Negro leaders alerted the masses to the fact that they were as liable to be drafted into service as any white man; that they were expected to be as patriotic and devoted to their country, laying down their lives, if necessary, even though in many areas they were deprived of their civil rights. They were still second-class citizens.

Under the Selective Service Act of 1917, over two million Negroes were registered and over three hundred thousand of them were called into active service, a larger percentage being drafted than among whites, because draft boards were less inclined to be lenient toward Negroes. They served chiefly in the Army, since they were barred from the Marines and up to that time had been restricted by the Navy to menial jobs.

The record of valor and courage which they made for themselves, in spite of being segregated into separate regiments, won them the respect and admiration of thousands of new friends. The 369th Infantry, volunteers from Harlem, New York City, was the first Allied army unit to reach the Rhine, and it was under fire longer than any other regiment of the A.E.F.

The miracle is that the Negro did prove himself a patriot in spite of the treatment meted out to him. America was his homeland, and he felt a deep obligation to her destiny, realizing that his own future was one with hers.

His civilian life within the United States was altered by the war, too. When factories converted into making war materials, they needed more workers than were available, and they had to employ Negroes. That started a vast migration of Negroes from the South to Northern cities, where they could hope for better wages and a chance to use their skills in industry.

Mrs. Bethune watched with alarm the migration of many of her own young people, because she realized that when the war was over they would be the first to be thrown out of work. She had traveled in Northern cities, and she knew that, while discrimination was not quite so severe as in the South, it was severe enough. Negroes were herded into squalid, inadequate quarters and forced to live in filthy slum conditions; they were barred from restaurants, hotels, theaters, and even some stores.

Her son was at Morehouse College in Atlanta, Georgia, and she wondered how he would respond to the lure of money. For his high-school training she had sent him to Haines Institute, where she herself had been so inspired by Lucy Laney. He was doing well in college, and she didn't want him to be tempted away from his studies. Happily for her, he remained at college during World War I; he joined the Reserve Officers Training Corps, a subdivision of the Army with units at colleges and universities to train younger men for future positions as reserve officers in the regular Army.

Mrs. Bethune raised funds and traveled for the Red Cross, sometimes lecturing on a few hours' notice, in Maryland, Virginia, and the District of Columbia.

As soon as the war was over, she was back giving her full time to the school and the community of Daytona. The school was forever in need of money, and the race situation in Florida demanded exquisite diplomacy. Contrasted with the generous white residents who gave constantly and fully of their support, advice, and encouragement were the bigoted whites who felt that the Negro must be kept in his "place," that any effort to help him was liable to encourage him to get "out of hand." The bigots resorted to extreme cruelties to enforce their ideas. No Negro was permitted on the peninsula side of town after dark. If he was caught crossing the bridge a few minutes before daylight to get to an early job, or returning a few minutes after dark because of some unavoidable delay, he was arrested, perhaps even beaten. Any white person known to have eaten a meal, or even drunk a cup of tea, with a Negro was socially ostracized. The slightest episode, or even an attempt to explain the episode, would bring about a Negro's arrest, the charge being that he was a "sassy nigger."

Although Mrs. Bethune was the soul of tact, patience, and understanding, because she did not want her school burned down or herself driven out of town, there were times when she saw the need of violating taboos, times when her courage was incredible in the face of the conditions in which she had to work.

"I don't know why they haven't killed me," she once confided to a white friend.

The bigoted element was on the alert, though, just to remind her that she must not go too far, and the Ku Klux Klan was an ever-present menace.

Shortly after the war and just before an election, the terrifying rumor reached the campus that the Klan was going to march that same night. Mrs. Bethune was in New York at the time, and Mrs. Keyser called the older girls together to explain the situation.

"Don't tell the younger girls," she cautioned them. "Do what you can to divert their attention so that they won't be too frightened."

Half sick with fear themselves, not knowing how much more than "march" the Klan would do, Mrs. Keyser and the young women remained on watch. Maybe this would be just a demonstration of strength, just a dramatic threat. Maybe no one would be killed this time. Maybe—

Night came, and the entire city was in pitch darkness; so was the school. The young students had been put to bed as usual, and the older ones stood at the front windows of Faith Hall to stare out into the night and watch and pray and wait. A tiny flicker of light in the distance! They were coming! The candle-like flicker grew larger as the parade drew near; it expanded into tall flames. Two men on horseback, carrying flaming crosses, led the procession. Others marched behind them on foot, all shrouded in white, wearing masks to conceal their faces. Even the most violent hate advocate did not want his face identified with this deed.

As the parade approached the entrance to the horseshoe drive that curved past White Hall, one of the riders lifted a horn to his lips and blew a weird, bloodcurdling blast that woke every student and awoke the watchers to their responsibilities. They found their voices and began to sing a hymn, persuading the others to join in, as the masked visitors moved slowly into the driveway and past the front entrance. The smaller children, too young to understand, thought the display was a Hallowe'en stunt, and they shouted and laughed and applauded.

The building watchman, a fellow to whom no one had ever paid much attention, calmly walked out of the front door of White Hall and stood proud and silent on the steps as the shrouded white men filed by him, continued on their way and out the other side of the drive, and disappeared into the night.

Praise God! This Klan visit had been only a warning. It was a warning to all residents of Colored Town not to appear at the polls on Election Day, and a promise of what would happen if so much as one Negro tried to vote.

Upon her return to Daytona, Mrs. Bethune listened unsmilingly to a report of the Klan episode. It was hardly news, and certainly no surprise. She had been educating the Negroes of Daytona for years and doing everything she could to encourage them to straighten their backs and demand their undeniable rights. There were bound to be repercussions. She, for one, intended to vote in the elections, and anyone who wished to join her was welcome to come.

The Klan had started in Pulaski, Tennessee, in 1866, when

a group of young men, some of them Civil War veterans, all penniless as a result of the war, depressed and in need of diversion, were sitting around one evening spoiling for ways to entertain themselves. They decided to form a club, and one of them said, "What about the Greek word *kuklos*, meaning circle?"

Laughing, joking, bandying comment about, they finally divided the word into Ku Klux and added Klan. What a mysterious title! They would call their club president the Grand Cyclops, their vice president the Grand Magi, their marshall the Grand Turk, and their treasurer the Grand Exchequer. They swore one another to secrecy. At first they spent their time making nuisances of themselves, dressed in long white gowns, white masks, and mounted on horses with muffled feet.

In another year the tragedy of Reconstruction had begun. Carpetbaggers were hurrying south to exploit the inexperienced, uneducated Negroes. Fear of being governed by the slaves they had themselves mistreated filled every white heart. When large numbers of Negroes began to be elected to state legislatures and to hold other public offices, white populations, in some instances in the minority, thought the end of civilization had come.

One night some Negroes saw a group of Ku Kluxers riding by in their white costumes along a lonely road and reported that they had seen a troop of ghosts. The idea caught on like an inspiration and spread from state to state. Harry the Negroes by playing upon their superstitious natures! Haunt them! Spread the idea that these shrouded night riders were really the ghosts of dead Confederate soldiers. Keep the Negroes from voting and holding office by terrorizing them.

The secret, cruel world of the Klan grew like a mushroom, and the atrocities it committed became more and more inhumane. It burned down the Negro schools and whipped and drove out of town those whites who had come South to teach in them. It beat, tortured, and killed Negroes, burning and looting their homes. It whipped whites who refused to join the Klan, and it kept up these outrages for years. Its worst crimes were committed during the ten years following the end of the Civil War, until "white supremacy" was established. Then the Klan's activities died down, and at one time it was reported to have been dissolved, but it never completely disappeared. In later years it seemed to experience a rebirth and extended its hate program to other minority groups, in some communities attacking Roman Catholics, in others Jews, burning fiery crosses in the night to persuade the undesired families to move out of town.

"Faith and courage!" was Mrs. Bethune's reiterated advice whenever the subject of the Klan was mentioned. "Patience and fortitude. Social changes cannot happen quickly. We are making progress."

The South found other ways and means to keep the Negro away from the polls on Election Day.

It used the poll tax, a fee of $1 or $2 that must be paid well in advance of Election Day by the person wishing to vote. This fee usually accumulates from year to year, sometimes with interest. To a sharecropper who earned as little as $100 a year, a fee of $1 was sufficient to keep him out of politics. Florida enacted a poll tax in 1885 and did not repeal it until 1937. Five Southern states still enforce a poll tax.

Another device for disfranchising the Negro is the "white primary." Primary elections, in which candidates are nominated to run for office in the general elections, are held separately by the two major parties. In a state where one party is overwhelmingly strong, usually the Democratic Party in the South, to win in the primary election is as good as being elected in November. In many Southern states the Democratic Party enforced the simple rule that no Negro could vote in Democratic Party primaries. This ruse kept the Negroes away from the polls in a long list of Southern states until 1944, when the United States Supreme Court ruled that the "white primary" was unconstitutional.

When the poll tax and "white primary" devices failed, there was still the Klan to intimidate the Negro who might be "spoiled" by too much education and decide to fight for his franchise.

Mrs. Bethune went right on educating, encouraging, and arousing the Negroes to think about their consitutional rights and their own betterment, and an Election Day never went by that she did not appear at the polls, with a group of dark-brown Americans determined to vote.

The Klan lost patience with her and rode again. The hooded figures, waving their burning crosses and blowing their weird horns, circled the drive in front of White Hall on election eve, and Mrs. Bethune was there waiting for them.

"Turn on every light in the school!" she boomed in her heavy, dramatic voice. "Let them know we're home!"

Wide-eyed, almost dumb with terror, the students crowded around her as light after light was turned on. She began to sing:

> "Be not dismayed whate'er betide
> God will take care of us!"

With quavering voices they joined in the hymn as seventy-five disguised marauders passed by the windows with their blazing emblems. Disguised? Well, when a man is exceptionally short and has an extra-large stomach, a sheet doesn't disguise him too well; or when a man is pigeon-toed, his sheet doesn't conceal the fact.

"The next morning," Mrs. Bethune reported triumphantly, "I was standing at the polling place at eight o'clock to vote with a line of Negroes behind me. They kept us waiting all day, but WE VOTED!"

Great Amazon of God behold your bread
washed home again from many distant seas.

*"For Mary McLeod Bethune" by Margaret
Walker*

13. *"Invest in a Human Soul"*

Daytona Educational Industrial
Training School was giving grades two years above high
school by 1921; and, since Mrs. Bethune was endeavoring to
obtain recognition of the State Department for the high
school, she changed the name to Daytona Normal and Industrial Institute. She didn't want to drop the word "industrial" from the title, because it was helpful in fund raising.
Patrons were more willing to support an industrial school
for Negroes than an academic one.

The school had several buildings by that time. The second
brick building, the library, stood across the street from White
Hall. Mrs. Bethune was not satisfied. She knew Faith Hall
had become an overcrowded firetrap, no longer a safe place
for the girls to sleep.

She stood in front of White Hall one day beside her secretary, Harold V. Lucas, and others of her staff, and pointed toward a stretch of swampy ground.

"I see a building," she said dreamily, her eyes half closed.

Her staff members looked at one another. Their "mother" had been working too hard for too long; she needed rest. There was no building, no money to erect one, and the ground wasn't fit for construction.

"I see a brick building," she reiterated. "Fireproof, with shower baths, sitting rooms, electric lights. I see a new home for my girls. I must go and write some letters."

No one argued with her when she was in a "building" mood, for all had learned long ago not to contradict her visions.

It was as though every dream to which she gave utterance was divine in origin and would be blessed by a divine coincidence to make it come true. Shortly after that nebulous conversation, Mrs. Flora D. Curtis, of Buffalo, a white tourist living out her remaining days in Daytona, made one of her regular visits to Second Avenue to buy carrots from the school garden. Crotchety, bothered by a delicate stomach that required freshly picked carrots and peas, Mrs. Curtis would fuss and fume over the selection of ten cents' worth of carrots, and then go to the office to pay Mrs. Bethune for them.

"Let her have what she wants," Mrs. Bethune always instructed the school gardeners, and no matter how bothersome Mrs. Curtis was, she always received polite treatment.

On her shopping trip to the school in 1921, she stopped in Mrs. Bethune's office and said, "This is my last year in Daytona. I won't be coming down here any more."

Mrs. Bethune expressed regrets.

"How much have I spent on carrots all these years?" asked Mrs. Curtis.

A scrupulous keeper of records, Mrs. Bethune told her the

amount immediately and gave her the date for each dime spent.

Mrs. Curtis could only stare in amazed admiration.

"Could you please send me your school paper each month?" she asked. "If anything happens to me, I may have some money."

Mrs. Curtis died shortly after that episode, and when her will was read, she had left the school $40,000, half the amount needed to build the new dormitory. This third brick building was named Curtis Hall in honor of the benefactor.

Not only did Mrs. Bethune keep a scrupulous record of every penny given to her, she took a deep interest in every individual who came within the orbit of her influence. Harold V. Lucas, her secretary, born in New Brunswick, New Jersey, and raised in Brooklyn, New York, had been severely injured in a football game. He was so badly injured that his body was completely rigid, and he was unable to bend his back or legs. He could stand or lie flat, but never sit. The verdict of the medical profession was that he must finish his days as an invalid, dependent upon others for his care and support. He naturally drifted toward the mild climate of Daytona and the slowed pace of the South, and, being a Negro, he found himself in Daytona's Colored Town.

With his college education and his training in commercial subjects he could be helpful around Daytona Normal and Industrial Institute, giving a little advice here and there, making suggestions. Of course, they must understand that he was incapacitated; he couldn't really *do* anything.

"Come into my office," said Mrs. Bethune. "As long as you know shorthand, I want to give you a letter."

She completely ignored the slow and dragging journey he made with the aid of his cane from the hall into her office, and as soon as the door was closed she began to dictate one letter after another until his book was full. He had no choice but to type them, and for the next eight years he was her personal secretary, the busiest man on the campus, and later he became an instructor in business administration.

She made him forget himself, made him a cog in the machinery, replaced his despair with hope, his defeat with self-respect. She was never too busy to reclaim a soul, and in her long life she reclaimed thousands.

Everyone who approached her with an idea or an act of generosity was made a partner in her lifework. When Mrs. Ada Lee knocked on the door of the school one day with a donation of sugar, flour, and tea, Mrs. Bethune was fired with a plan, and she talked it over with Mrs. Lee at once. Women could be organized into Bethune Circles, groups of ladies who would make practical contributions to the school such as silver, dishes, sheets, new curtains. These items constantly needed replacing. No sooner was one bought than another had worn out. This idea was as successful as all her others, and soon there were ten chapters in operation.

Mary McLeod Bethune stood alone at the age of forty-eight, with thousands of others depending upon her wisdom and spiritual strength. Her husband had died in 1919, and her son was a grown man with his own life to live. If at times she longed for the strength of another person to lean upon, there was no hint of it in her personality except for an occasional reference to "Leaning on the Everlasting Arms."

She had been watching the fate of Cookman Institute, a men's college in Jacksonville, Florida, that was trying without too much success to compete with two other colleges nearby. In spite of having taken in boys many years before, her own school until then had been largely a girls' school, and she wanted it to become coeducational. Cookman was run by the Board of Education of the Methodist Episcopal Church North. In 1923 plans were put into action to merge the two colleges, and in March 1925 they were completed. All the real and personal property of the Daytona Normal and Industrial Institute was deeded over to the Methodist Episcopal Church, and the new coeducational school was called Daytona Cookman Collegiate Institute.

"Mr. Chairman," Mrs. Bethune said to her Board of Trustees, "this is a very sacred moment for me. I realize what it means to have a dream, a vision, and to put that vision into operation, to see it come to a reality."

In compliance with her wishes, the Board of Trustees passed the resolution necessary to accomplish the merger, and Mrs. Bethune thanked them from the bottom of her heart.

"I want you to use it," she told the Methodist Church, "as an institution that stands for all that is great and noble in manhood and womanhood. I want you to use it as a life that has been given for the cause. I yield it, Mr. Chairman, with God's blessings upon this work, with His sure protection around all that we have done; take it, develop it, use it!"

The merged schools had to continue giving high-school work, because in those days high-school instruction offered in public schools for Negroes was of such poor quality that the students were not ready for college when they presented themselves for admission.

After the merger, Mrs. Bethune sought a few strong men to join her staff, among them Professor John C. Wright, former president of Edward Waters College in Jacksonville, who came to the college as vice president. He brought with him Miss Bertha Loving, now Mrs. Benjamin Mitchell, as his secretary, and she later became Mrs. Bethune's secretary. When her own work permitted, she helped with the voluminous correspondence that Mrs. Bethune always turned out, and between the young Bertha Loving and the mature Mary McLeod Bethune a rare friendship and deep understanding developed.

Bertha Loving had heard that Mrs. Bethune was a severe woman, and she went to meet her with fear and trembling. Furthermore, Miss Loving had bobbed hair, at a time when hair bobbing was still very daring. She was sure Mrs. Bethune would disapprove of her hair, so she wore a hat for the interview and marched into Mrs. Bethune's office to meet her fate.

"I'm Bertha Loving."

Mrs. Bethune wheeled around in her chair, looked at the visitor, and said, "You look capable. You will get along."

The young girl felt at ease immediately, because Mrs. Bethune left personality out of the conversation and began to discuss the work of the school. Later on, when they were better acquainted and Miss Loving had become Mrs. Bethune's full-time secretary, Mrs. Bethune did remark that she did not like bobbed hair.

But Miss Loving found her new chief anything but severe. Severity was saved for slackers. Mrs. Bethune proved to be generous and compassionate, deeply feminine, yet possessing strong executive qualities. She was interested in men, enjoyed their company, and liked to impress them in a woman's way; but she could think, plan, and organize in a completely effective manner.

Slim, pretty, and stylish, Bertha Loving could have wanted the free hours and gaiety that young girls crave, but she found that to work for Mary McLeod Bethune was to become engulfed in a labor of love that eclipsed every other interest. By that time Mrs. Bethune had a house of her own on the edge of the campus, and her secretary moved right into the house with her, to be on twenty-four-hour call.

Mrs. Bethune could work until midnight, sleep three or four hours, and awake as refreshed as though she had slept the clock around. She would sometimes call her secretary at four in the morning and say, "Come and bring your book."

Startled out of a sound sleep, Miss Loving would look at the clock, terrified for fear she had overslept, and think, "Doesn't she realize that it's only four o'clock in the morning?"

She soon learned that during those early morning hours Mrs. Bethune did her clearest, most creative thinking. When the rest of the world was silent, some of her most constructive ideas were born. Without a dime she would start to plan, and the result would be Cookman Hall, the brick boys' dormitory; or the Trades Shop, where the men students could learn to be carpenters, shoemakers, electricians, auto mechanics, and radio workers.

The happy-go-lucky young men students who thought at first that they would have an easy life under a woman president soon learned to respect her split-second punctuality, her phobia for cleanliness.

A meeting scheduled to begin at eight o'clock began at eight o'clock, whether or not anybody was present.

If she saw a scrap of paper on the campus lawn, she would march toward it and scoop it up in an angry hand.

"How could you walk past that piece of paper and not *see* it?" she would demand of anyone within earshot. "How could you *look* at it and not pick it up?"

They soon learned, too, that when she appeared in a white dress instead of the customary dark one, she was in a militant mood and about to begin a ruthless inspection tour. One glimpse of the white-garbed figure coming across the lawn, and students would disappear into their rooms to pick up strewn clothing, or faculty members would vanish to straighten out supply closets.

With a larger administrative staff to help her after the merger, Mrs. Bethune was able to give more time to activities outside the college. On a speaking engagement in Palatka, Florida, she was delighted to discover on the same platform with her a young Negro teacher fom Mississippi with a group of her students who were to sing in Mrs. Bethune's honor. She had done the same thing herself for so many years that she made it her business to meet the young woman, Arenia C. Mallory.

"Where is your school? Tell me more about it! How many students do you have?"

Arenia Mallory, handsome, tall, spoke with a rich, low voice. She was from Illinois and as a young girl had gone back into the most hopeless part of the South, the semi-barren farm areas of the Delta section, where large Negro populations paid seventy-five per cent of the taxes and received in return a minimum of opportunity, or none at all. There she took a teaching post in the Saints Industrial School in Lexington, Holmes County, Mississippi.

Mississippi, in the heart of the black belt, is the only state in which the Negro population exceeds the white. Mississippi delta land has the richest cotton soil in the country; with cotton goes sharecropping for the Negro, and with sharecropping goes poverty, sickness, ignorance, discrimination. Even today Mississippi allots $1.00 for each Negro child's education, as compared with $5 for every white. Negro students have a shorter school year than the whites, because they are needed in the fields.

Recognizing Miss Mallory's talent immediately, Mrs. Bethune encouraged her with praise and advice, corresponded with her regularly, signing her letters "Mother."

When Saints Industrial School celebrated its twelfth anniversary, Mrs. Bethune traveled to Mississippi for the occasion, and she was met at the railroad station by a thousand barefoot boys and girls who had arrived on muleback, in carts, on foot. When Mrs. Bethune stepped from the train, Arenia Mallory stood on top of an express wagon and led her students in a song to welcome the illustrious visitor, and the train waited until the song was finished.

Tears streamed down Mrs. Bethune's face.

"Arenia Mallory," she said, "someone just like you came into the backwoods of South Carolina when I was a barefoot girl like these little girls and found me one day and gave me my chance."

Under Mrs. Bethune's persuasion Miss Mallory has remained at her post for twenty-five years. The thirty thousand Negroes who had no high school a quarter of a century ago now attend a school that can accommodate five hundred of them at a time and that plans to add junior-college grades to its curriculum.

"Mrs. Bethune has been a great inspiration," is Miss Mallory's explanation. "Equal to my own mother, and I am only one of many over whom she has watched."

That is why she has stayed in the heart of Mississippi with the children who once were without hope "down behind the sun."

In 1924, a group of Mrs. Bethune's friends and admirers presented her with a trip to Europe, and she spent eight happy weeks wandering through Italy, Switzerland, Germany, Holland, Belgium, France, England, and Scotland. In Rome she was received by the Pope and given his special blessing. When she reached London, she found that the Lord Mayor and his wife were waiting to receive her, and in Edinburgh, the Lord Provost and Lady McLeod. She came back to Daytona refreshed and happy, her vision widened by all the new sights and personalities she had experienced.

The name of her school was changed once more, when her trustees protested that her own name should be memorialized. She consented, and the school became Bethune-Cookman College.

At her half-century mark, Mary McLeod Bethune was really just beginning her ascendancy as an outstanding American educator and a leader in humanitarianism; her influence was being felt in wider and wider circles, and the force of her personality was reaching individuals in every walk of life all over the country. Although her figure had grown heavier and a streak of white showed in her jet-black pompadour, fifty years did not seem to have reduced her limitless supply of energy. She could still outwork her associates, with no regard for herself.

When the hundred-mile-an-hour hurricane of 1928 swept through a curved path over the Bahamas to Palm Beach and northward over central Florida, she dropped everything and rushed to West Palm Beach to help the Red Cross in its relief work. Land was flooded, giant palms uprooted, homes destroyed, over a thousand persons killed and thousands more left injured and stricken.

"I have dealt with epidemics of influenza and other diseases," she reported, "but I had never been faced with a situation like that. The storm had been drastic. We went out and tried to relieve the people and get them from under the debris, but the thing that was striking to me was to see those great trucks coming in from the outlying areas with bodies piled upon them like logs of wood, white and black. An effort was made to separate the bodies, but there wasn't time, and big plows turned over the soil and buried them seven and eight to a grave. It was an experience that I hope will never be mine again, but I thank God that I was able to be there and to help the Red Cross set up its machinery to bring relief to the sufferers. It was a time when people forgot creed and class and color, an opportunity for great humanitarianism, and we were all alike looking to the God who was controlling the affairs to give us the belief and wisdom and common sense and unity of service to meet the requirements of the hour."

Exhausted and shaken by her experience, Mrs. Bethune returned to Daytona to find that the storm had sent the river flooding across the land, and when the waters receded, one entire quadrangle of the campus had been inundated. A new problem always seemed to give her new strength, and she telephoned to a contractor.

The washed-out area would require ten thousand loads of sand to refill it, he told her.

"How much?" she asked, not having any money at all.

"A dollar a load."

"Very well, start delivering the sand. We will use volunteer workers to spread it."

She called in her secretary and said, "I must get off a letter to Mr. Gamble, Dr. M. M. Kugler of Cleveland, Dr. Charles F. Goss of Cincinnati, Mr. Harrison Rhodes of Cleveland, Dr. John Frothingham."

She named several more who had been her devoted supporters in the past, and reminded her secretary that each letter must be sealed with the thought that divine love takes care of everything. That was Wednesday; by Monday evening she had the entire $10,000.

That same year found her in California for the annual meeting of the National Association of Colored Women, of which she was president. She had been active in this group for several years, ever since the day its chairman had allowed her to speak to the meeting on behalf of her school in Florida. She had made such a profound impression on that first occasion that the president, Mrs. Mary Church Terrell, hurried to her after the meeting and said, "You have just the characteristics to make you a good president of the National Association of Colored Women, and I hope I'll live long enough to see the day when you will be."

Mrs. Bethune and Mrs. Terrell laughed together in later years over the way Mrs. Bethune was dressed at that time. She felt no concern for anything but her students in Florida. Any hat, any dress, would do for her. When she was re-elected to the presidency at the business session in Oakland, California, in 1928, Mrs. Bethune was dressed with more style. Moving out into public life had forced her to think of the value of her appearance, and with her deep sense of the dramatic she sometimes dressed deliberately to cut an impressive figure, affecting a huge picture hat or a long white cape. She developed the habit of carrying a cane, and it became as much a part of her personality as her pompadour.

After the Oakland sessions, the ladies adjourned to a huge meeting and reception in Los Angeles, where Mrs. Bethune was the principal speaker.

Whenever Mary McLeod Bethune spoke, the most vibrant qualities in her personality became evident. She would stand silent for a moment, head tilted slightly upward, as though waiting for a message from above. Eyes half closed, she would intone the first words, and her audience saw the missionary, the spiritual messenger, heard the deep, rich resonance of a voice that was almost bass. Using short sentences and clear-cut thoughts, moving slowly at first, building up a gradual crescendo until she reached a high-speed excitement that carried everyone with her on a wave of emotion, gradually slowing at the close of her speech, leaving her listeners with a deep sense of benediction, Mrs. Bethune stretched out her expressive hands and closed them quickly as though to turn off the sounds of her own voice.

She had pleaded eloquently for underprivileged colored girls. She wanted more help for them; they were human souls in distress.

The association members waited in silence for a moment, then burst into round after round of enthusiastic applause.

With the speakers on the platform sat a modest white woman, aging hands folded in her lap. Too discreet to show any emotion, she smiled happily all the time Mrs. Bethune was speaking.

A delegation came forward, bringing a bouquet of flow
which they handed to Mrs. Bethune, who turned and l
them in the lap of the shy old lady.

This guest of honor was Mary Crissman, the Qual
woman who believed in giving one-tenth of her income
charity and who had provided Mary McLeod's scholarshi
to Scotia Seminary and to Moody Bible Institute. She ha
lived to see her investment return dividends a thousandfol
Few eyes were dry.

"Invest in a human soul," Mrs. Bethune begged her au
dience. "Who knows? It might be a diamond in the rough."

Let the knowing speak
Let the oppressed tell of their sorrows,
Of their salt and boundless grief.

"Adjuration" by Charles Enoch Wheeler

14. *Adviser to the President*

As Mrs. Bethune's personality unfolded to reveal her true greatness and she moved inevitably out into the main stream of national affairs, she was in wide demand as a speaker, and she used her eloquence at every opportunity to plead for interracial good will.

"There is no superior or inferior race," she said again and again.

It was a mistake to judge Negroes by those on the bottom layer.

"The Negro has made his contribution to American culture and to the world, and this contribution is represented through the Negro's patience, tolerance, forgiveness, and love. . . . In order to know which way a tree is growing, we must watch the upper branches: those of the race who have accomplished something and are leaders. The race should be judged by that group rather than the masses who have not had their chance to develop."

She gave generously of her time to every organization that was working for the promotion of racial understanding.

The National Urban League was one of these. Started in 1910 by a group of white social workers to improve conditions of Negroes in New York, its motto "Not alms but opportunity," the National Urban League has expanded its membership and responsibilities until today it has branches in nearly sixty cities manned almost entirely by Negro social workers. It helps unemployed Negroes to find work, persuading both labor unions and white employers to accept them; it operates day nurseries for the children of working mothers, neighborhood clubs and playgrounds, and does what it can to raise living standards in Negro quarters of American cities.

Mrs. Bethune became affiliated with the National Urban League just after World War I when, in 1920, she was elected to its Executive Board to take the place of Mrs. Booker T. Washington, who had died a short time before. The other members of the board found her to be, not militant, as they had feared, but wise, patient, persuasive, and possessed of exceptional vision where the future of race relations in America was concerned. They sometimes sat fascinated as she won over an opponent in a debate on policy, making her adversary suggest the very idea she wanted, convinced that it had been his own all along.

Mrs. Bethune was a diplomatic link between the Negro world and the white, and whenever a white individual or group asked her what the Negro wants, she would reply without hesitation:

"Protection that is guaranteed by the Constitution of the

United States and which he has a right to expect; the opportunity for development equal to that of any other American; to be understood; and finally, to make an appreciable contribution to the growth of a better America and a better world."

The National Association for the Advancement of Colored People was another group to which Mrs. Bethune gave her help. It, too, began in New York, a year before the National Urban League, but the N.A.A.C.P. concentrated most of its efforts on legal work to obtain civil rights for the Negro through the courts. Since its founding, the N.A.A.C.P. has made a brilliant record for itself. Between 1915 and 1950 its attorneys won twenty-eight out of thirty-one cases before the United States Supreme Court, decisions outlawing the white primary, ending segregation laws in many cities, forbidding the use in court of confessions obtained by torture, eliminating Jim Crow regulations on interstate trains and buses, permitting Negro students to enter many white colleges.

Mrs. Bethune's friendship with Walter White began when she became a vice president of the N.A.A.C.P. in the late 1930's, since he was executive secretary of the organization. Walter White's blue eyes, blond hair, and white skin draw stares of amazement when he announces that he is a Negro. Coming out of Georgia in the Deep South, having narrowly escaped being lynched on more than one occasion, he came North after World War I to take a low-salaried post with the N.A.A.C.P., and ultimately he rose to be its chief executive officer. His entire life has been one of dedication to the Negro cause.

The 1920's, that had been years of prosperity—thoughtless years of plentiful employment, high wages, high prices, careless living, talking pictures and radios—were not to last; in the fall of 1929 the stock market crashed and the whole

American economy began a downward plunge into a deep and tragic depression. Bankruptcy, unemployment, actual starvation faced countless people, and individuals such as sharecroppers and tenant farmers, who lived in a precariously narrow margin even in good times, were in desperate straits. The depression left youth all over the country without opportunity or hope. If there was no hope for even the upper levels, what about Negroes?

As the depression reached its lowest point, the nation faced a Presidential election in 1932, and an overwhelming change was made. The Republican Party, which had been in power for twelve years, was swept out of office, and the Democratic Party, with Franklin Delano Roosevelt at its head, went into the White House.

American Negroes since Civil War days had more or less identified themselves with the Republican Party, because it was Lincoln's party and because they were most severely discriminated against in the overwhelmingly Democratic states of the South. The advances they were able to make under Theodore Roosevelt strengthened the bond, although it was weakened again by the loss of many of those gains under subsequent Republican Presidents. When the second Roosevelt was elected to the Presidency under the banner of the Democratic Party, Negroes did not hope for much; but after he had been in office a short while, they began to hear talk of a "new deal."

Mrs. Bethune was accustomed to conferring with Presidents by then; in November 1930 she had been invited by President Hoover to the general session of the White House Conference on Child Health and Protection, and the following year to the President's Conference on Home Building and Home Ownership.

Franklin D. Roosevelt, with his extraordinary gift of being able to pick exactly the right person for a job, asked her to serve on the Advisory Committee of the National Youth Administration that was just then being set up.

Even though she did not meet him during her entire first year with N.Y.A., while it was being formed, she knew she had moved into the sphere of influence of a great personality. She worked in a state of excitement and elation, helping to bring N.Y.A. into being.

N.Y.A. was really a junior Works Progress Administration, and its purpose was twofold: to give part-time employment to students in schools, colleges, and universities, so that they could continue their education; and to give both training and full employment to idle young people who were not in school —a helping hand extended to the youth left hopeless by the depression.

The unforgettable day came when Mary McLeod Bethune was to sit in conference with the President of the United States and give him a report on minority group activities of the N.Y.A.

"Dear Lord, help my people; help me to help my people," she had prayed fervently for years, and on this day her prayers were to be answered.

Aubrey Williams, the National Youth Administrator, was also present at that conference. A tall, thin, dour-faced ex-pastor, a Southerner devoted to the Negro cause, he sat quietly in his chair as Mrs. Bethune spoke directly to the President.

"In many parts of the South the fifteen-dollar or twenty-dollar check each month means real salvation for thousands of Negro young people," the daughter of slaves explained. "We are bringing life and spirit to these many thousands who for so long have been in darkness. I speak, Mr. President, not as Mrs. Bethune but as the voice of fourteen million Americans who seek to achieve full citizenship. We want to continue to open doors for these millions."

Tears were coursing down the President's cheeks when she finished. He leaned across the table and grasped her hands in both of his.

"Mrs. Bethune," he said, "I am glad I am able to contribute something to help make a better life for your people. I want to assure you that I will continue to do my best for them in every way."

The room was still when he finished speaking, and a few minutes later the conference dispersed.

Aubrey Williams placed a hand on Mrs. Bethune's shoulder as they walked out of the room together and said, "Thanks to you, a marvelous impression has been made tonight for the cause we all represent."

Although that was her first meeting with the President, Mrs. Bethune was no stranger to the rest of the Roosevelt family, for the President's mother and wife had both entertained her at luncheon in their home just after her return from Europe. Several Southern women had been present at the luncheon. Mrs. Bethune, ever the soul of tact and consideration, hesitated, and Mrs. James Roosevelt took in the situation at a glance.

"That grand old lady," wrote Mrs. Bethune, "took my arm and seated me at the right of Eleanor Roosevelt, in the seat of honor! I can remember, too, how the faces of the Negro servants lit up with pride when they saw me seated at the center of that imposing gathering of women leaders from all over the United States. From that moment my heart went out to Mrs. James Roosevelt. I visited her at her home many times subsequently, and our friendship became one of the most treasured relationships of my life. As a result of my affection for her mother-in-law, my friendship with Eleanor Roosevelt soon ripened into a close and understanding mutual feeling."

Shortly after she began her work with the President, a

signal honor was paid to Mrs. Bethune by the N.A.A.C.P., announced in a letter from the organization's secretary:

May 29, 1935

Dear Mrs. Bethune:

It is with profound pleasure that I have the honor to advise you that the Spingarn Medal Award Committee has selected you as the 1935 Medalist.

May I extend both official and personal congratulations to you upon this well-merited recognition of your devoted services. . . .

Ever sincerely,
WALTER WHITE
Secretary

Mrs. Bethune laid the letter down carefully after she had read it. Deep within her still lurked the barefoot cotton picker who so desperately wanted to learn to read and who wept so profusely when she was told there would be a school for her. That little girl still went wild with joy when fortune smiled at her, still fell on her knees and thanked the sky. The dignified lady of sixty smiled and touched a buzzer to summon her secretary so that she could dictate her reply.

Dear Mr. White:

Your letter has completely overwhelmed me. I just cannot find words to express the deep gratitude, the humility, the wondrous encouragement—the many, many emotions which flow over me when I think of this signal consideration.

This year has been such a hard, hard one and we are just going into the last month of it. It is so significant my burdens are thus lightened by this recognition of whatever service I have been privileged to render. I never feel worthy of honors, but they are great stimuli to my strength and faith and courage.

May success continue to crown the work of the
N.A.A.C.P.

> Sincerely yours,
> MARY McLEOD BETHUNE

The Spingarn Award is a much-coveted gold medal presented each year by the N.A.A.C.P. "for the highest or
noblest achievement by an American Negro during the pre-
ceding year or years." It has been given to such outstanding
Negroes as George Washington Carver, the scientist; Ro-
land Hayes, the tenor; James Weldon Johnson, author and
diplomat; Carter G. Woodson, historian and founder of
the Association for the Study of Negro Life and History;
Walter White, Executive Secretary of the N.A.A.C.P.;
Marian Anderson, contralto; A. Philip Randolph, labor
leader; William H. Hastie, governor of the Virgin Islands;
Dr. Percy L. Julian, research chemist; William E. Burghardt
DuBois, author and founder of the Pan-African Congress;
Ralph J. Bunche, the United Nations mediator in Palestine,
and winner of the Nobel Peace Award in 1950; and other
notables.

Mrs. Bethune traveled to St. Louis at the end of June to
receive, before a vast audience in the municipal auditorium,
the gold medal on which was embossed a figure holding the
scales of justice in one hand and the sword of courage in the
other.

Her acceptance speech, "Breaking the Bars to Brotherhood," carried her listeners along on its spiritual message, as
her strong, protruding jaw seemed to protrude a little farther
and her heavy features tightened with determination. "To be
worthy of being included in the illustrious group of Spingarn
Medalists . . . one must respond to the stimulus of this occasion with a spirit of rededication to service, reconsecration
to the needs of the people. . . . the National Association for

the Advancement of Colored People has spent its efforts almost wholly in clearing the way for the race; in breaking the dead branches from the paths of opportunity. . . . The law of life is the law of cooperation. . . . If we would make way for social and political justice and the larger brotherhood, we must cooperate. Racial cohesiveness means making a rope of all of the achievements of those who have had education and advantages, until we reach the lowest man in the lowest stratum of the masses. Unless the people have vision, they perish. . . ."

Her audience strained forward as she increased her speed and accelerated her emotional appeal. Many were hearing her for the first time, and while they had known of her miraculous achievements they had not been exposed to her dynamic personality before.

Miss Josephine Roche, then Assistant Secretary of the Treasury, was the next speaker, and when she finished, two large bouquets were sent to the platform, one presented to Mrs. Bethune and the other to Miss Roche. There was tremendous applause, and as if by inspiration the two women, one black and the other white, turned and embraced each other. Walter White said he had never been so deeply moved.

After the conference Mr. White and Miss Roche returned to New York together, and while they were having dinner on the train, Miss Roche said:

"That is the first time I ever saw Mrs. Bethune, and I was tremendously impressed with her. What do you think of her for a more important post in the National Youth Administration?"

"Mrs. Bethune could fill any post with dignity and ability," was his enthusiastic reply.

Josephine Roche had been assisting President Roosevelt to set up the N.Y.A., and she had her eye out constantly for talent. She left the St. Louis meeting convinced that Mrs.

Mary McLeod Bethune 160

Bethune could handle far more responsibility than had been demanded of her by her work on the advisory committee.

When Mrs. Bethune received an invitation to another conference with the President, her heart gave a leap. How much more would he be willing to do for the downtrodden? How much more would she be allowed to do?

She prepared for the trip to Washington with so much excitement that when she rushed into the railroad station in Daytona Beach to purchase her ticket, she found herself in front of the window marked, "For Whites." There wasn't time to correct the error; she mustn't miss her train. So she pushed a $20 bill through the grill and spoke brusquely to the clerk:

"Give me a ticket to Washington, D.C., and do it quickly!"

He hurriedly obeyed, and not until she had boarded the train did he realize what he had done.

"Say!" he called to a companion. "Why, I believe she was colored. Say, I forgot!"

When Mrs. Bethune reached her destination, she hurried directly to the offices of Aubrey Williams. His usually dour face lighted up with a smile when she entered, and he greeted her with the wonderful news:

"The President has decided to set up an Office of Minority Affairs of N.Y.A., and you are to be its administrator."

Sobered and humbled by the immensity of the responsibility, Mrs. Bethune took a startled step backward and protested, "I can't do that. I have to look after my college."

"I'm afraid you'll have to," he told her. "Do you realize this is the first such post created for a Negro woman in the United States?"

She sank down into a chair as her exceptional vision lighted up the vistas of the future, and she nodded her agreement. She had overcome so many insurmountable barriers in her life; surely she could do this, as long as her faith held. Yes, she would have to do it, because she was paving the way for other Negro women who came after her.

Later in the day the President received her and Mr. Williams, and she was able to say:

"Thank you, Mr. President, for your thoughtfulness and deep concern for my people and all minorities that need help. You have been most gracious in permitting me to share so deeply in such a great cause. In accepting this appointment, I assure you that I shall give it the best that I have and shall follow very closely the guiding hand of our great administrator, Aubrey Williams, who is giving so fully of himself for this cause that is so dear to your heart."

"Aubrey," said the President, "Mrs. Bethune is a great woman. I believe in her because she has her feet on the ground; not only on the ground, but deep down in the plowed soil."

Her new Washington post proved a blessing, because there was a salary attached. One of the first economies she had enacted at the school when the depression struck had been to discontinue her own salary completely. Other teacher and staff salaries had been reduced, and there had been times when she had not known how she would meet her payroll. Now she could send a large portion of her salary to Daytona every month to defray school expenses, never thinking to keep anything for herself.

The first years of the depression had not seriously affected her school otherwise, because there had been no building going on. In 1934 a new brick Faith Hall had been put up, as well as a completely fireproof science building with the motto over the doorway, "All Science Points Toward God," the latter a gift of the General Education Board.

In Washington lived her old school chum, Teets, still devoted to the older girl who had looked after her at Scotia, and whose close warm sympathy proved a welcome relief from the intense strain of nationwide office.

As soon as she took up her duties, her administrative ability was felt, and young American Negroes, on learning that they had a champion in the federal government, lifted up their heads and began to hope, flooding her desk with touching letters:

"I am a colored boy 19 years old and am in very bad need of work. Please help me get a place in the National Youth Administration. They say that it helps poor boys and girls like me."

Or, "I have been reading about your great work and I've heard the program over the radio. I need your help so very bad and I have finished high school and want to enter college."

Or, "I've been out of school for five school terms. I have no father and my mother isn't able to work regular on account of a run-down condition. So you see I must have work, so please help me. . . ."

The N.Y.A. had a local administrator in each state, and Mrs. Bethune traveled all over the country, visiting the various schools and projects that had been set up for Negroes, investigating new situations that ought to have a project.

One of the first steps she took before going into the field for the N.Y.A. was to call a conference in Washington of all Negro leaders, so that she could have the benefit of their combined experiences; and out of that conference grew many of her plans for Negro youth for the next ten years.

Under her supervision six hundred thousand Negro young people were benefited. N.Y.A. work projects employed nearly twenty thousand in clearing playgrounds and parks, building dormitories and schoolhouses, repairing roads, and helping in forest conservation. They took pride in the fact that what they received, they had earned. The money in their pockets wasn't dole. Those in schools were able to learn trades in the Resident Vocational Training Projects in agriculture, shop work, dressmaking, nursing, child care, in exchange for their board and tuition.

To travel thirty-five thousand miles, speak at more than forty meetings in twenty-odd states in a single year, was a typical record for this woman in her sixties. Every step was painstakingly reported in her column, "From Day to Day," in the Pittsburgh *Courier*:

April 15, 1937

I left Washington at six o'clock on Wednesday after a full day's work in my office. I arrived in Louisville at 9:15 in the morning. . . . I immediately started my tour of the projects and activities of the N.Y.A. in the city of Louisville.

We first visited a very promising project for girls at the community center where they were engaged in all types of sewing, rug weaving, and home management. From there we visited another project for young women at the Municipal College. . . . My visit to Kentucky was at an opportune time, as the Negro and white teachers were holding their educational meetings. I had helpful conferences with the presidents of the colleges and principals of the high and elementary schools.

At six o'clock I was at dinner with the Iota Phi Lambda girls at a very fine restaurant owned and controlled by Negroes. . . . At 8:30 I was escorted by Mr. Salyers and Mr. Brown to the meeting place of the K.N.E.A., to find the block impassable with an overflowing house and people trying to crowd in. . . . By force the men opened up a narrow passage to allow me to get to the platform. . . . At 10:30 my

> hostesses Georgia and Alice Nugent served tea . . .
> and discussed vital topics of the day. . . . I then
> threw myself on the bed and at 2:25 A.M. I took a
> train for Detroit. . . .

And she lived that kind of schedule for ten years, still finding time through it all to worry about, and work out, administrative problems of Bethune-Cookman College.

After four years in the Washington post, she reported in
her column:

> From Texas to the Carolinas and from Florida to
> New England I have repeatedly said of our pro-
> gram: "The N.Y.A. is building a new emancipation
> for Negro youth from the despair of denied opportu-
> nity for training, for guidance, for work and for
> healthful recreation. Almost 40,000 young Negro men
> and women have been assisted by N.Y.A. to attend
> high schools, colleges, and universities all over the
> land. A veritable army of youth marching to an educa-
> tion under the N.Y.A. banner who might have been
> left out of the parade. . . .

Whenever political machinations in Washington threatened
to curtail the funds for N.Y.A., she would hurry back to the
capital to confer with the President and Mrs. Roosevelt, and
soon a reassuring sentence would appear in her column:

"Seems a real possibility for extension of our fine
work. . . ."

The President trusted her and depended upon her, and
once he paid her the compliment, "I am always glad to see
you, Mrs. Bethune, because you never ask for anything for
yourself."

Congress at one point was determined to whittle costs, and
a $100,000 graduate-training fund in the N.Y.A. appeared
doomed.

"We mustn't allow that to happen," Mrs. Bethune said to Aubrey Williams.

"You'd better speak to the President about it," he advised her.

She hurried to President Roosevelt's office, and because she knew how busy he was, she began to tell him quickly and briefly about the dangers of bringing such a fund to an end. She became so excited and so concerned that she jumped out of her chair and shook her finger in his face, shouting:

"Think what a terrible tragedy it would be for America if by this action by a committee of Congress, Negroes would be deprived of the leadership of skilled and trained members of their race!"

Horrified to find herself speaking so harshly to the President of the United States, she apologized. "Oh, Mr. President, I didn't mean to become so emotional."

The President smiled graciously and tapped the tip of his long cigarette holder against an ash tray.

"I understand thoroughly, Mrs. Bethune. My heart is with you."

The following week Congress renewed the full grant to the National Youth Administration program.

The friendship between Mrs. Roosevelt and Mrs. Bethune deepened, too, and they appeared often on the same speakers' platform; so often, in fact, that many affectionately commented that America really had two first ladies: Lady Eleanor and Lady Mary.

When Mrs. Bethune began to cough in the middle of one of her speeches, Mrs. Roosevelt, who was on the same program, left her seat, poured a glass of water, and brought it to Mrs. Bethune, standing over her while she drank it. Those who witnessed the scene never forgot that gesture of humility and service coming from one of the most outstanding women of the world.

If anyone in those years had asked Mrs. Bethune what she did, she would have replied:

"As a teacher, school administrator, and Director of the Division of Negro Affairs of the National Youth Administration, my work has been, for the most part, entirely with youth. I know something of their problems, their ambitions, their hopes and desires. To watch them grow, expand, and develop is one of the great joys of human gardening and engineering. There is no greater job on earth than that of assisting with the development of human personalities. I work with youth."

Stand erect and let your black face front the
west.

"Close Your Eyes!" by Arna Bontemps

I5. *Nationwide Influence*

While she was her busiest in the
early formative years of the National Youth Administration,
the founder of Bethune-Cookman College created her second
great idea: The National Council of Negro Women.

Traveling all over the United States, consulting with every
topnotch Negro leader, discovering all sorts of Negro-
betterment organizations, some of them overlapping their efforts, she realized that Negro women and their local groups
needed a clearinghouse for their efforts. In 1935 she called together representatives of a dozen or more women's associa-
tions and laid before them her plans for the National Council.
Its membership was to represent all communities: civic,
church, labor, education, professions; and its goal would be

to improve opportunities in every field: better housing, better working conditions, higher standards of living, equal educational opportunities, civil rights—to remove the second-class label from the American Negro.

The idea caught on and spread like wildfire; the membership rolls mounted; and the National Council grew into a powerful organization that today has reached and influenced nearly a million women from every state in the Union. It has been responsible for bringing to public attention a host of brilliant and cultured Negro women such as Dr. Dorothy Boulding Ferebee, one of Mrs. Bethune's physicians who ultimately succeeded her as president of the National Council; and Mrs. Edith Sampson, the Chicago attorney who in 1949 went on the round-the-world trip of America's Town Meeting of the Air, and the following year was appointed an alternate delegate from the United States to the United Nations General Assembly, the first Negro to hold such a post.

The early days of the Council were not easy, for, among other things, it had no adequate place of its own in which to meet, and no funds to speak of. Mrs. Bethune heard that a house on Vermont Avenue in Washington, D.C. was for sale, and she and two or three others found that they could scrape together from their personal funds the $800 necessary for the down payment. Ten thousand dollars more would be needed.

"You should never have involved yourself or the Council in such a debt," she was told. "You know you don't have that much money."

She had been hearing that kind of advice all her life. "You can't go to Scotia Seminary; there isn't any money." "You can't build a girls' dormitory; there isn't any money." "You can't buy the house for the Council; there isn't any money."

Others might forget God, but she never did; and she never attempted anything without requesting divine help. She was in Chicago at the time, and she said to her friends in a quiet, confident voice:

"I think I shall ask Marshall Field for the money. With God's help, I shall be able to persuade him."

"What? You don't even know him."

"That's all right. Now, I want the rest of you to start praying; pray all the time I am gone; and don't stop until I get back. Pray that I shall be able to convince Marshall Field that he ought to help me buy the house."

Off she went to his office, and what transpired between Marshall Field III, heir to the department-store millions, and the passionate crusader is not known. In spite of his wealth, Marshall Field was a hard worker all his life, one who had a keen interest in child welfare and other causes. His selfless disposition showed in a sensitive, finely featured face and a kindly manner, and he must have enjoyed interviewing Mary McLeod Bethune. In any event, she returned to her friends an hour later in triumph, flourishing a check for $10,000 under their doubting noses. Her deep spiritual integrity had won again!

The year following the founding of the National Council, Mrs. Bethune was elected president of the Association for the Study of Negro Life and History. The founder of the Association, Carter G. Woodson, had been the son of slaves in Virginia, and he had had difficulties similar to Mrs. Bethune's in obtaining an education. He began his career as a teacher, first in high school and later in Howard University, doing writing and research in the history of the Negro in his spare time. When he discovered that few, if any, publishers would accept books on Negro subjects, he organized his own publishing company and the association of which Mrs. Bethune became president in 1936.

The presidency was really an honorary position, since Dr. Woodson, as director, did the bulk of the work. Mrs.

Bethune's name brought it tremendous prestige, and her vast following among people of modest means attracted to the Association a large volume of small donations. Until her election, Dr. Woodson had had to depend upon large grants from a few wealthy sources such as the Carnegie Corporation, Laura Spelman Rockefeller Memorial, and the Rockefeller Foundation. Mrs. Bethune's influence helped to create a broader financial base upon which to rest the Association's work.

One more year brought the Drexel Award, when Xavier University in New Orleans, Louisiana, at its commencement exercises presented Mrs. Bethune with a gold medal "for distinguished service and devotion in the cause of humanity and the betterment of her fellow men." Xavier University was founded by the Sisters of the Blessed Sacrament especially for work among Indians and colored people.

During her years in Washington with the N.Y.A., Mrs. Bethune became one of the most influential women in the United States, and to the Negroes a beacon light. She brought them together, crystallized their efforts, gave them a sense of direction.

Realizing how successful her first conference of Negro leaders had been, she organized another such meeting in 1937, naming it the National Conference on Problems of the Negro and Negro Youth. She was able to call on high places for support of the project; Mrs. Roosevelt was the principal speaker at the opening session, and Aubrey Williams was another; altogether about a hundred prominent persons blessed it with their presences. President Roosevelt sent a message of encouragment.

When Mrs. Bethune addressed that packed auditorium, cane in hand for dramatic effect, she spoke proudly: "We find that twelve million colored people are beginning to get together and think courageously upon the problems confronting them. We are doing this not as individuals but as an entire group. We are presenting our cause properly to the administrative powers of this country, then looking them squarely in the face. . . ."

This land is ours by right of birth,
This land is ours by right of toil;
We helped to turn its virgin earth,
Our sweat is in its fruitful soil.

"Fifty Years" by James Weldon Johnson

16. *A Thirty-five-Year Reckoning*

Thirty-five years had passed since the young searcher after her mission in life had stood in the midst of Colored Town in Daytona and had chosen it as the place for her school. They had been years filled with heartache, worry, humiliation, and even grief; they had also been years full of triumphant achievement. Bethune-Cookman was a full-fledged junior college in 1939, having been able to drop its high-school courses four years earlier, and the rolling lawns of its campus, the brick buildings, the well-dressed, well-mannered young people who hurried from one class to the next were the creation of a single great soul—Mary McLeod Bethune.

On Sunday afternoon, February 18, 1940, a star-studded list of American leaders gathered on the campus to celebrate the thirty-fifth anniversary of the founding of the school, the ceremony concluding a three-day program.

Mrs. Roosevelt traveled all the way from Washington to speak at this anniversary, and although she had heard detailed reports about the college, her surprise was as genuine as everyone else's who visits Bethune-Cookman for the first time. Her automobile rolled slowly through the tree-shaded streets of Daytona, past wealthy homes, and across the tracks to the Negro quarters. As it proceeded along Second Avenue she saw first the hovels typical of the wrong side of town; then suddenly Second Avenue was transformed, lined on both sides with lawns and brick buildings.

In her column, "My Day," the First Lady wrote of her visit:

> Until I went over the plant I never realized what a really dramatic achievement this junior college is. It administers to the needs of 100,000 Negroes from Daytona south, and it takes 250 students. The object is to train leaders who will return to their communities and serve their people in whatever line of activity they have chosen as a life work. Thirty-five years ago Mrs. Bethune began with five little girls. The first land was bought with the first $5 earned. This land up to that time had been part of the city dump, a portion of the city known as "Hell's Hole."

Because of the huge crowds that were expected and that did arrive for the Sunday afternoon worship, Mrs. Bethune decided to hold the service out of doors, even when she was cautioned that the sky threatened rain.

"The chapel will be too small today. I've decided to hold the meeting out of doors."

"But Mrs. Bethune, with Mrs. Roosevelt speaking—if it rains—"

Persons of high rank and influence were prevailed upon to argue with her, but it was no use. When Mrs. Bethune made a decision, it stuck, and argument only brought the bulldog jaw out an extra inch. "Stubborn," someone called her, not remembering that the very chapel in question had been created out of pure stubbornness.

When Mrs. Bethune, Mrs. Roosevelt, Aubrey Williams, and other speakers mounted the outdoor platform and faced the throng, Floridians who knew perfectly well that rain would fall before the day was another hour old held their peace. What would be, would be.

The sky was courteous to Aubrey Williams, but after Mrs. Roosevelt had been introduced, the first big drops splashed on the makeshift planks. Mary McLeod Bethune, the stubborn, the woman of unshakable intent, did not yield even to the elements. She turned to a student sitting near her, handed her an umbrella, and snapped, "Here; go hold this over Mrs. Roosevelt's head."

If Mrs. Roosevelt minded giving her address in the rain, she never said so; and after the meeting and the brief shower were over, she strolled about the grounds with the founder-president, listening intently to her plans for the future.

Mrs. Bethune was still dreaming, still planning. The library was inadequate, too small a building and not nearly enough books. She and others were now busy raising funds for a Harrison Rhodes Memorial Library.

Harrison Garfield Rhodes, the writer, best known for his dramatization of *Ruggles of Red Gap*, had been a friend of the college for years and had remembered it generously in his will. Rather penurious in his living, his excuse had always been that he wanted to save as much money as possible for his bequest to the college. Whenever Harold Lucas went to his house to take dictation, Rhodes would hand him exactly as many pieces of stationery as would be needed for the letters, and he would caution Lucas not to waste any by making typographical errors.

Friends of Bethune-Cookman were always remembered, and after several years of fund raising, the new library was erected and named for Harrison Rhodes. Today it is one of the largest and most complete libraries available to Negroes in the Southeast.

A second reckoning loomed large in that milestone year when Mary McLeod Bethune, who had been called "indestructible" by one of her physicians, startled everybody with the news that she must undergo an operation. She had been distressed by a severe asthmatic condition for years, and the doctors of Johns Hopkins Hospital in Baltimore, where she had gone for a complete checkup, decided that an operation would have to be performed on her nasal passages.

Solicitous inquiries flooded in from every point of the compass; those who had been depending upon "Mother" Bethune for years were suddenly terrified by the prospect of losing her; Teets hurried from Washington to look after the patient, making the final arrangements for the operation and staying with Mary Jane constantly all the time she was in Johns Hopkins.

In spite of the almost universal affection in which she was held, in spite of her high rank in the national government, Mrs. Bethune was confronted by the specter of Jim Crow the minute she set foot inside the hospital. Johns Hopkins had no private rooms for Negroes in the surgical or medical divisions, where she belonged, but did manage to find one for her in the gynecological department, a special gesture because she was so exceptionally outstanding. Frequently, colored people of note are placed in rooms by themselves and made to feel like private patients, but actually it is done as a cover-up.

Mrs. Bethune had never been a spokesman for herself; she was a torchbearer for others. She asked for a Negro surgeon when she discovered that every nurse and doctor on the staff was white.

"There are two distinguished Negro physicians in the city," she persisted. "Can you let them participate, or at least observe the work?"

She won her point. Both men were invited, and ever since that time there have been Negro doctors on the staff of Johns Hopkins.

During her six weeks' stay she taught lesson after lesson. When one of the young nurses called her "Mary," the southern way of addressing a Negro, she rebuked the girl and explained that she was *Mrs.* Bethune.

"I have trained hundreds of girls like you. You are not my friend or relative, that you can call me by my first name."

The girl apologized and the story went all over the hospital.

Shortly after she entered the hospital, a white basket, taller than a chair, filled with an assortment of handsome gladiolas, was presented to her; it carried Mrs. Eleanor Roosevelt's personal card. Mrs. Roosevelt sent flowers from the White House greenhouse twice a week, and each time the nurses would vie with one another for possession of the White House seal on the box.

Mrs. Bethune kept a careful diary of her six weeks in the hospital, and while she must have experienced real discomfort, even severe pain, at times, she left hardly any record of complaints. Each day's log began with a cheering note, "Thank God for light." Or, "Thanks for life, thanks for morning." "Glorious Day." "All my trust in Thee." There followed a record of the visitors, services, progress. Teets appeared day after day in the diary, stayed with her until she was settled, brought her her breakfast, answered her mail, tidied her room, changed the water on her flowers, "came with her cheer and sunshine."

The patient lay back on her pillow, her benign and kindly face usually glowing with a smile, as her forceful personality affected the entire establishment and drew a host of visitors to her bedside. Highborn and low, young and old, every color and nationality, they trooped by to pay their respects and express their fears for her safety. "A Japanese friend called." "People flock to get a chance to see me. I wish we could admit them all, but we cannot."

"A young man entered my room and said he had heard of me and my kindness to people and he wanted me to give or lend him $5,000. He said he knew a person who had done what I had done was worth a million dollars. He frightened me. But I soon got him straightened out, gave him some good advice, and sent him on his way."

"A wire from my students asking me to listen in to the 'Wings Over Jordan' program, that they will be listening in meditation with me. Our hearts met at the altar."

Meetings were held at her bedside, so that they would have the benefit of her help. "We had a good conference on N.Y.A. affairs. The day closed."

She had been overtired and overweight when she entered the hospital, and could not have her operation until her physical condition satisfied the doctors. So the stream of friends, admirers, committees, and conferences flowed on while the doctors supervised her care.

On April 18 she wrote: "My diet nurse with my breakfast—small glass orange juice, one small egg, one-fourth glass milk, one-half slice toast. The pounds must go. I am 190 this morning. Mail, letters, and cards from all over. God bless my friends!"

At last, in the middle of May: "The operating nurse came. Everything was in readiness. Dr. Young and Dr. Rhetta, our

Negro doctors, observed the operation. Dr. Polvogt was the surgeon. I was not fully asleep. I was sufficiently conscious to know what was going on, but I never had, in my opinion, such a patient, tender, painless surgeon. The operation was a success. Long hours of restlessness and occasional dull pains," she admitted.

During the operation the surgeon repeated the error of the young nurse who had addressed her by her first name.

"Mary, turn your head," he said.

With the instruments in her nose, she couldn't do anything but obey, although the next morning when he visited her room she explained to him that she was Mrs. Mary McLeod Bethune.

"Please forgive me, Mrs. Bethune. I didn't mean to be discourteous," came the sincere apology.

It was his custom, he added lamely, to call all of his colored patients by their first names.

That same afternoon he sent her a huge basket of flowers, because he had been so impressed by her complete cooperation. Never in all the time he had operated there had he ever sent a patient flowers, one of the nurses told her.

As soon as she was pronounced out of danger, Mrs. Bethune lost interest in herself again; she had really been concerned only with being allowed to continue working. As she lay convalescing, she could see from her window the entrance to the School of Preventive Medicine across the street, and one day, when a class of nurses, all of them white, filed out, Mrs. Bethune sighed and said, "I do hope that the day is not far off when some of my girls will be in that group."

Creature of faith though she was, a thread of sorrow began to run through her diary when she heard reports on her radio of world affairs.

"The condition of the war seems serious," she wrote in April, and at the end of May, shortly before she was dismissed from the hospital: "The shocking news of the morning is the surrender of Belgium. What will come next?"

War clouds, never completely cleared away after World War I, had been gathering over Europe for several years. The tide of militarism was rising slowly but steadily under Mussolini in Italy and Hitler in Germany.

When Mrs. Bethune dictated the simple question: "What will come next?" Germany had already begun to spread her borders, having invaded Poland the previous fall, and Great Britain and France had followed that act by declaring war on Germany. The surrender of Belgium was soon followed by the sweep of German troops across northern France.

Mary Bethune was just beginning to get about again when France surrendered.

She shuddered when she realized how far the hate virus could spread, how much racial animosity already existed in America and how quickly it could increase. The outcome of this new strife would determine the future of America's largest minority group. There was no difference between the lynching of a Negro in Georgia and the torturing of a Jew in Berlin.

She must get back to work, increase her schedule, cover more meetings, write more letters, watch over her young people, raise the campaign against hatred.

When a nurse or doctor cautioned her, "Mrs. Bethune, please try to rest. You haven't fully recovered. You must think of yourself," she would look up, bewildered. Think of herself? Now?

> . . . . . . in spite of all—
> *We will not hate.* Law, custom, creed and
>   caste,
> All notwithstanding, here we hold us fast.
> Down through the years the mighty ships of
>   state
> Have all been broken on the rocks of hate.

> *"Self-Determination" by Leslie Pinkney Hill*

17. *Two Protests*

A year before her illness, Mrs. Bethune and other leaders had taken public issue with the powerful and long-established Daughters of the American Revolution, when Marian Anderson, whose voice Toscanini once said is the kind that comes once in a century, was denied permission to sing in Constitution Hall in Washington, D.C.

Miss Anderson's agent wrote to the D.A.R. to arrange for the use of the hall, and he was advised that it was already reserved for the dates he requested. On writing again to suggest several other evenings, he was firmly advised by the daughters of the Founding Fathers of American liberty that

no dates were open. The reason was obvious enough: Miss
Anderson was a Negro.

By 1939 Marian Anderson was an international figure who
had thrilled audiences on both sides of the ocean with her
three-octave range, her rich vocal tones, and her rare emotional renditions. Returning from a triumphal tour of the
Continent, where she had given concerts in London, Paris,
Belgium, Holland, Austria, Russia, Poland, Italy, Spain, and
Finland, and where she had made close friends of such persons as Mr. and Mrs. Jean Sibelius, she began a concert tour
of her own country, appearing with the symphony orches-
tras of Boston, Buffalo, New York, and Philadelphia. But
Constitution Hall, the only building in the national capital
big enough to house the vast audiences that Miss Anderson
attracted, was denied to her by the D.A.R., who owned it,
with the grim implication: "Jim Crow."

The entire city of Washington was strictly segregated;
Negroes were not permitted in theaters, restaurants, hotels, or
other public places, and they lived in segregated areas
throughout the city.

The thirty-one-year-old contralto-soprano, who had been
born to poverty in Philadelphia and had won a place for herself in the highest musical circles of the world, was no
stranger to race prejudice. She had experienced it many times
in her life, always meeting it with the same calm patience.

A storm of protest rose up around her, however. Leading
musicians such as Walter Damrosch and Deems Taylor said
they hoped "that this amazing action reflects the opinion of
some irresponsible official." Writers, churchmen, and other
musicians joined in the outcry. Jascha Heifetz, the violinist,
said he felt ashamed to play in Constitution Hall, and Mrs.
Eleanor Roosevelt announced in her column that she had resigned from the D.A.R.

Residents of Washington organized a Marian Anderson

Citizens Committee, calling a mass meeting to protest the action, and Mrs. Bethune hurried to that meeting of fifteen hundred persons of every imaginable background.

"I have nothing much to say," she told them. "I just want my person—I just want myself—I just want every ounce of Mary McLeod Bethune to stand here against any injustice that confronts the Negro. . . . Fellow citizens, listen to me this afternoon—there can be no peace without justice. . . ."

The meeting adopted a resolution calling on the D.A.R. to rescind its action and allow Marian Anderson to appear. The Daughters stood firm in their resolve. No Negroes in Constitution Hall!

The matter would not rest, and soon the idea began to grow that Miss Anderson give an open-air concert in Washington. Walter White said that the suggestion had come from Fiorello H. La Guardia, then mayor of New York City. In any event, it proved an effective one, and arrangements were made for Marian Anderson to give a free concert on Easter Sunday afternoon before the Lincoln Memorial.

Seventy-five thousand persons assembled to hear her sing; crowds were packed into every space before the memorial and down both sides of the lagoon. Harold L. Ickes, Secretary of the Interior, acted as master of ceremonies and spoke briefly on racial tolerance.

When Miss Anderson appeared between the huge Grecian columns, walked down the steps, and approached the microphone, humble yet dignified, unassuming and beautiful, a hush fell over the vast assemblage. She stood with eyes closed, as she always does when she sings, and waited for the first notes of the piano. Her voice defies description, and the heart must have been hard indeed not to be touched that day. She opened her program with "America," then sang "O Mio Fernando" by Donizetti, "Gospel Train," Shubert's "Ave Maria," and "My Soul Is Anchored in the Lord."

Music was Miss Anderson's language, and the only protest she made to the action of the D.A.R. was in the closing piece in her concert, when she sang the spiritual, "Nobody knows the troubles I've seen. Nobody knows but Jesus."

Not until four years later did the D.A.R. relent, even to a degree, and invite her to sing within its sacred chambers, when it was planning a series of war-relief concerts. Miss Anderson replied that she would sing for them if they did not "Jim Crow" the hall and would not ban her future appearances there. After a long, embarrassing pause the D.A.R. gave in on the first point but not on the second. They would allow Negroes and whites to sit side by side on the night that she sang, but they could not make any guarantees as to the future. Hoping that one victory would lead to another, Miss Anderson agreed to the compromise and sang to a mixed audience of thirty-eight hundred. Mrs. Roosevelt was present in one of the boxes, with Mrs. Henry Morgenthau and Lady Noble, whose husband was chief of the British Admiralty delegation. The entire proceeds of the concert were donated to United China Relief, and Miss Anderson turned over her own fee to the fund.

As the war in Europe spread, the attention of America was to be called again and again to the way it treated its minority groups, particularly its largest minority, the brown-skinned Americans.

American industry stepped up its production to furnish Great Britain and her allies with ships, aircraft, and weapons for the fight against Germany and Italy, to aid China in the fight against Japan, and to meet the demands of increased national defense. The step-up in production meant an accelerated demand for workers, and, as had happened in World War I, southern Negroes again migrated north in large numbers to such manufacturing centers as New York, Detroit, Chicago, and San Francisco.

In the twenty years between World War I and World War II they had raised their literacy rate to ninety per cent. They had developed their own universities and colleges, turning out thousands of graduates. They were no longer the traditional superstitious farm hands, easily frightened by white-hooded night riders, but doctors, nurses, teachers, mechanics, bankers, scientists, writers, artists, craftsmen; and they wanted an equal chance to use their training.

"Having come, in three hundred years in America," said Mrs. Bethune from behind her N.Y.A. desk in Washington, "through most of the hardships and sufferings, oppressions and denials that mark the experience of the white race for over a thousand years, the Negro in America faces a crucial period in his history. He is now at the crossroads where he is ready to turn down the road, where he will forever drop from his shoulders the burdensome mantle of slavery and assume the rights and privileges of a full Christian life and citizenship with his fellow Americans. . . . Negroes have been surrounded by a vicious circle—they are not used in certain jobs because they are not trained, and they are not given an opportunity for training because they are not employed in such jobs. . . . Today the Negro faces the problem of participation in national defense. It may seem strange to some of you that thirteen million Negroes, confronted by every conceivable obstacle and hindrance, should display such loyalty to America and such gratitude for American citizenship that they are fighting for a chance to fight. It is no secret that the program for national defense has not lowered its bars sufficiently for the proper inclusion and integration of Negroes into it."

In New York City, one of "Mrs. Bethune's boys," Asa Philip Randolph, a Cookman Institute graduate, decided to go into action and organize an effective protest. A Floridian by birth and the son of a poverty-stricken Negro clergyman,

Randolph had worked his way up until he became the most prominent Negro labor leader in the country. As a youngster he had done every kind of odd job to help keep his family from starvation. After graduating from Cookman, he worked as a waiter, an elevator operator, and a porter. Just before World War I he and a few others started the Brotherhood of Sleeping Car Porters, and for the next twenty years he devoted his efforts to building up the membership and influence of the union, until the Pullman Company, which had refused time and again to negotiate, was at last forced to sign a contract granting higher wages and shorter hours.

When addressing a meeting in Chicago of the Ladies' Auxiliary to the Brotherhood, Mrs. Bethune described Randolph as "a poor barefoot boy, knocking at the doors of opportunity to get sufficient training for the gallant leadership of his people that he has so ably demonstrated. When we read the pages of integrated labor, we place his name at the top of the list of Negroes who have waged through blood and fire the battle for the entrance of Negroes into union ranks of labor. The name of A. Philip Randolph will forever stand as a fearless, heroic leader who did not let suffering or hardships stop him from waging war for human justice."

Randolph saw that Negroes were not being allowed their fair share of jobs in defense plants, and he went up and down the streets of the Negro sections in New York and Chicago, asking the single question: "What are you going to do about it?"

He talked to shopkeepers, businessmen, housewives, students.

"What about it?" he asked again and again. "Do you want a job in a defense industry? We need to let the government know that Negroes are willing to give their lives for their country, but we also want to have the right to earn a living in industry at home."

He found them willing to respond, and before long he had rallied a huge following.

"We will march on Washington," he told them as their excitement mounted. "We will rise up from every part of the United States and march on the national capital in mass protest and demand fair treatment in industry."

The March-On-Washington Movement, with A. Philip Randolph as its national director, grew at a high rate of speed as volunteer workers joined the ranks, laboring far into the night without pay to write and print literature, address envelopes, and perform the mountain of clerical work that had to be done to operate the campaign. This peaceful revolution was their first attempt at mass expression, and it must succeed. When thousands and thousands of them, rallied by the literature and speeches, rose up to converge upon Washington, the government would have to listen.

In less than four months the efforts to organize an army of marchers had reached such proportions that President Roosevelt called Randolph and Walter White into conference. Being in such close touch with the grave international situation, realizing that at any moment the United States might become involved in the war as a participant, the President knew full well how dangerous it would be to ignore or misdirect a movement involving thirteen million Americans. And he realized, too, how justified their protest was.

"You can't do it this time," he said to Randolph. "You mustn't go ahead with your march."

The adroit labor leader was forced to tell the President that the march would most certainly take place unless something was done to prevent it, something that would mean justice for Negroes. After considerable thought, the President agreed to act, and he kept his promise, writing Executive Order 8802, which abolished discrimination because of "race, creed, color, or national origin" in both industry and the federal government.

Order 8802, issued on June 25, 1941, was the crowning achievement of the March-On-Washington Movement, and when Randolph and his associates were informed of it, they agreed to call off the march.

The first direct result of the order was the creation of the Federal Committee on Fair Employment Practice, composed of seven consultants, two of whom were Negroes. This group went to work immediately to persuade labor unions and employers to accept Negroes, to hold large public meetings and rallies to arouse public good will toward Negroes, and to write a fair-employment law and persuade Congress to enact it.

Mrs. Bethune received the news of 8802 and the F.E.P.C. with joy and excitement, and a few weeks later, at a patriotic rally in Cincinnati, she said, "The first bright ray in the dawn of that new day broke through the clouds of denied opportunity and despair when our grand President issued an Executive Order outlawing discrimination in defense industries and defense training and creating a committee to enforce his decree. For the first time since Lincoln issued the Emancipation Proclamation, freeing us from the bonds of slavery, an executive order, work in the form of law, has issued from the White House to open the doors a little wider for Negroes."

Less than six months after that conference, the tragedy of Pearl Harbor drew America into the war.

Then the setting sun
   Burned a ghastly red:
Blood of young men
   Too soon dead.

"Green Valley" by Dorothy Vena Johnson

18. *Global War*

Wars are despicable things! How much better off civilization and the world would be if we could forever remove the causes of war!" These were Mrs. Bethune's words as she saw America plunge deeper and deeper into armed conflict, saw the lives of her young people changed overnight. From the moment when, on that grim December 7, the news flashed over the United States that the Navy had been bombed, she rededicated herself to humanity and country; her long workday was increased, her travels intensified, her concern for her school deepened.

Bethune-Cookman, like all the other Negro colleges, was full of young people eager to join up: in the Armed Services, in industry, in civilian responsibilities. She intended to do all she could to open opportunities for them, and her strategic position in the N.Y.A., keeping her in touch with Negro youth all over the country as well as with the government, made it possible for her to do a great deal.

The shock of Pearl Harbor, followed by the talk that America was going to war to end totalitarianism and oppression in other lands, awakened the national conscience to the state of affairs at home. There was oppression and discrimination within our borders; America's own hands were not clean. The kind of discrimination that was being practiced against the Negro was creating a divided and weakened country, and a weakened democracy might not be able to win a war against such great powers as Germany and Japan. Even the bigots were reached by this logic.

Alert Negro leaders read the temper of the times. They had been keeping alive the March-on-Washington Movement membership with meetings and tolerance campaigns, and they were ready to act when the time was right. If America was willing at last to extend a helping hand to her minorities, they were ready to reaffirm their loyalty to America and challenge her to give them, in return, union membership, a chance to serve in the Army and Navy, jobs in war plants.

The March-on-Washington Movement convened gigantic mass meetings on Negro rights in the Coliseum in Chicago, in the Municipal Auditorium in St. Louis, and in Madison Square Garden in New York City. The rally in New York City was the largest, with twenty thousand persons packed into the hall. Top-flight Negroes were present to bring their messages of encouragement: Reverend A. Clayton Powell, Jr., Dr. Channing H. Tobias, a member of the National Board of the Y.M.C.A.; Walter White, of the N.A.A.C.P.; Lester Granger, Executive Director of the National Urban League; and, of course, Mrs. Bethune.

"Your being here tonight is a new experience to America,"

she told them in her heavy, melodious voice. "Throughout the history of your life in this country—three hundred years—you have been regarded as a patient, submissive minority . . . . you had no rights. The Supreme Court held that you were chattels, like any horse, or plow, or iron pot. . . . Then came your emancipation. Still you were patient, experiencing discrimination, injustice, segregation, and denials of equal opportunities. Here and there a clarion voice rose above the rumblings of injustice. . . . But the pall of a slave experience still hung over the masses of our people. They had a right to speak out, but dared not speak. Today a new Negro has arisen in America. He is here tonight in Madison Square Garden. He is you!"

She was past retirement age and only five feet six inches high, but on the speakers' platform she loomed tall and strong and had the power to impart that strength to others, making them rise out of their seats and cheer until the rafters rang.

The walking stick was always in her hand, although she had no physical need of it, and when asked why she used it, she replied gaily, "I carry it for swank."

On she went from meeting to meeting—Washington, Chicago, San Francisco, Cincinnati—to Nashville, Tennessee, in April 1942 to receive the Thomas Jefferson Award, a gold medal presented by the Southern Conference for Human Welfare, for "outstanding service in the field of human welfare in line with the philosophy of Thomas Jefferson."

"She has fought for freedom and democracy for all the people of the South with devotion and courage, particularly in her services in developing our youth for greater service to their country," the citation stated.

Her doctors warned her to slow down. Her asthma attacks were becoming more severe, sometimes lasting as long as two hours, leaving her prostrate and exhausted. She always promised to obey, then forgot the promise as quickly as it was made. So many needed her! Off she rushed to Concord, North Carolina, to speak at the seventy-fifth anniversary of Scotia Seminary. The school that had made her a first-class citizen was now Barber-Scotia College and could boast of ten buildings. She looked at the double flight of stairs that had once startled her, walked through the areaway from Graves Hall to Faith Hall, and mounted the platform in the chapel.

"I have stood here and said many little speeches, not once, not twice, but scores of times," she told the new generation about to go to war.

Wherever she traveled, even in the South, she saw taboos crumbling away in total mobilization, because they had become more inconvenient to the white man than to the colored. Often she herself broke taboos deliberately when she thought it necessary, because the years had brought her privilege, and she could walk in with her cane and sit down where no Negro had sat before. She broke some segregation laws because she didn't have time to worry about them. Hurrying through the Atlanta, Georgia, railroad station with a party of Negro and white companions, she came up the long stairway from the tracks to the landing, the white waiting room straight ahead, the colored on the right. In order to reach the ticket window she would have had to go out of doors and around to the other entrance. There wasn't time. She marched straight through the forbidden room, and when a policeman stopped her, she bestowed a gracious smile upon him and said, "Oh, I am all right," and went on. Amused, the man turned to a porter and asked, "Is she colored?"

Another time she was sitting in the airport of the same city, chatting with a white soldier to pass the time, when an Atlanta policeman came up and said, "You can't sit here."

She replied, "I am quite all right, thank you."

The young white soldier snapped at the policeman, "Let

this woman alone. This is the sort of thing we are fighting for, and this woman is fighting with us for that end."

She thanked God she had been allowed to live long enough to hear those words.

The spring after Pearl Harbor, Congress passed a bill creating the Women's Army Corps, and two days later it was announced that Mrs. Oveta Culp Hobby of Texas had been appointed director. The representatives of several Negro groups and lobbies in Washington objected strenuously to her appointment, fearing that, since she was a Southerner, Negro women who wished to enlist would not receive fair treatment. The National Council of Negro Women asked the Secretary of War to appoint Mrs. Mary McLeod Bethune as Assistant Director of the WAAC, later known as the WAC.

Oveta Culp Hobby, wife of a former governor of Texas, and Executive Vice President of the Houston *Post*, belonged to the new South, the younger generation that wanted to see an end to the old divisions, and she generously accepted Mrs. Bethune when she was loaned by the N.Y.A. to be a Special Assistant to the Secretary of War, to aid in the selection of Negro WAC officer candidates.

Ambitious as both Mrs. Hobby and Mrs. Bethune were, they had to face the fact that the WAC was part and parcel of the United States Army, and, in the Army, segregation was the order of the day. They had to accept the idea of separate units and do everything possible to see that Negroes received the same treatment as whites.

Mrs. Bethune was really in on the ground floor when she went to Fort Des Moines to consult with Lieutenant Colonel Hobby in selecting the first officer candidates. Her influence reached far beyond the bounds of the Women's Army Corps. When she saw a situation she didn't like, she spoke up; and when she spoke, she was heard in high places. If she saw a Negro youth being discriminated against in war industries, or denied equal and adequate training in schools, her complaints were carried by the leading newspapers.

Her young people worshiped her and, naturally, expected her to work miraculous changes the minute she appeared on the scene; and she would have to counsel patience again and again.

There came a day, though, at the end of 1942, when she had to listen to her doctors and heed the pressure of her sixty-five years. Even though the N.Y.A. had closed its doors when so many young people were absorbed into the war effort and unemployment vanished, she could not continue being President of a college in Florida, President of the National Council of Negro Women in Washington, and adviser to the director of the WAC all over the United States.

The decision of what to give up was not an easy one to make. But because she realized that her federal responsibilities were paving the way for other Negroes to succeed her, and because she knew how much President Roosevelt and others depended upon her, she relinquished the task closest to her own heart—her school—resigning the presidency to a successor, Professor James A. Colston, and becoming President Emeritus.

"Today Bethune-Cookman College has fourteen modern buildings, a campus of thirty-two acres, and six hundred students learning how to lead useful, happy lives," she said on "We, the People," one of her countless broadcasts. "But there is still much to be done. I'm sixty-five years old now, and my doctor wants me to rest. But I'll never rest. Never as long as there is a single Negro boy or girl without the chance that every human being deserves—the chance to prove his worth."

In the year in which she resigned as president of her college, to give full time to the war effort, Bataan peninsula had fallen, the Japanese were already in control of Singapore, Indo-China, the Philippines, Thailand, Burma, and the Aleutians of Alaska, and were advancing into China. On the European continent, Germany was penetrating deep into Russia. It was a dark year, but through the darkness she could see a persistent ray of light. She knew that the concerted effort of vast numbers of the new generation, both Negro and white, was bearing rich fruit when the U.S. Navy announced that it would accept Negro enlistments in categories other than mess attendants. Another two years of agitation, and Negro women were admitted to the WAVES and SPARS.

The war years transported hundreds of thousands all over the United States who had never traveled more than a few miles in their lives. Northerners were sent into the South to military camps or industries; Southerners went north. Americans were given a chance to become acquainted with one another, and a new understanding was born, not of despair but of knowledge. Twentieth-century America had neither the time nor the patience for eighteenth-century customs.

No one will ever really know how much Mrs. Bethune did for the war effort, because her contribution cannot be measured. It reached far back into the N.Y.A. years, when her remarkable foresight built equipment and trained personnel needed during the war. At her insistence, an N.Y.A. unit at Crispus Attucks High School in Indianapolis had installed a casting and forging unit and a machine-tool and foundry unit. Young men trained at that machinery stepped into essential jobs with the Link Belt Company, to make treads for tanks. The Higgins Industries drew N.Y.A.-trained craftsmen from Xavier University in New Orleans, to produce P-T boats. There were similar instances in South Charleston, West Virginia, with radio-electrical workers; Jacksonville, Florida; Houston and Dallas, Texas.

She worked on a special committee with Walter White and Channing Tobias to help in setting up hospitals, and they succeeded in preventing segregated hospitals in New York

City and Chicago. General George C. Marshall sent her on a special inspection tour of the general hospitals to check on morale, attitude, and conditions.

Beloved, respected, and honored, Negro and white alike seemed to compete with one another to do her honor with radio appearances, banquets, testimonials, and medals. The summer of 1945 found her at MacDill Field in Florida on the reviewing stand with Colonel R. J. Burt, Commanding Officer of the Engineering Aviation Unit Training Center, while the parade held in her honor by men of the E.A.U.T.C. passed in review. She was dinner guest at the mess hall of the squadron afterward, where the men presented her with a huge bouquet of flowers.

Probably the least known and most important of all her war services was the tremendous amount of correspondence she carried on with servicemen and women, giving them encouragement, advice, and inspiration. Any troubled young heart could come to "Mother" Bethune, and by the end of the war she was the pin-up girl of thousands.

Let a new earth rise. Let another world be born. Let a bloody peace be written in the sky. Let a second generation full of courage issue forth; let a people loving freedom come to growth. Let a beauty full of healing and a strength of final clenching be the pulsing in our spirits and our blood. Let the martial songs be written, let the dirges disappear. Let a race of men now rise and take control.

"For My People" by Margaret Walker

19. *Working for World Peace*

Long before the end of the war, international leaders began to lay the groundwork for peace, beginning in August, 1941, when President Franklin D. Roosevelt and Prime Minister Winston S. Churchill met "somewhere in the Atlantic" on board a British battleship to write the Atlantic Charter. The Atlantic Charter guaranteed that Great Britain and the United States respected the integrity of other nations, large and small, and pledged themselves to work for a peace in which all nations would have the means of "dwelling in safety within their own boundaries, and which will afford assurance that all the men in all the lands may live out their lives in freedom from fear and want."

After Pearl Harbor the tides of war mounted higher and

higher, drawing in even the South American countries, and in January, 1942, the United Nations came into being, when twenty-six countries met in Washington, D.C., to declare their support of the Atlantic Charter and to combine their efforts to defeat the Axis powers.

The days that followed were filled with human tragedy and waste of property; not until 1943 did the world see any real hope. In that year the United Nations began to chalk up victories in the Pacific; a front was established in Africa, from which Italy was occupied; and Allied air bombings hammered away at German factories.

On D-Day, June 6, 1944, five A.M. London time, the Allied forces crossed the English Channel and began their invasion of Normandy, and within a few weeks they had retaken Paris.

In August another conference was convened at Dumbarton Oaks, a private estate in a Washington, D.C., suburb, to which representatives of the four big nations—the United States, Great Britain, Russia, and China—came to draw up preliminary plans for a world organization to maintain the peace that they hoped would soon be established. Between the time of the writing of the Atlantic Charter and the conference at Dumbarton Oaks, Roosevelt, Stalin, and Churchill had met at Teheran, and after Dumbarton Oaks they met again at Yalta. Strategies of war and further groundwork for peace by world government had to be worked out.

By the spring of 1945 General MacArthur's troops had recaptured the Philippines, Allied victory on the continent of Europe was not far off, and plans for a conference of forty-six (ultimately fifty) nations to draw up a permanent charter for the United Nations were well under way. This conference, too, was to be held in America, and San Francisco was selected as the site, an excellent choice, since it is a liberal city in which persons of all colors could be received graciously in hotels, restaurants, theaters, and public conveyances without embarrassing discriminations.

President Roosevelt may have had a second reason for selecting San Francisco, since most of the delegates would arrive from their respective countries in New York City or some other Eastern port and would thus have a chance to travel across the entire United States. He arranged to have the delegates' trains proceed from New York to Washington, then northwest to Chicago, southwest to southern California, and up the coast to San Francisco. He wanted them to see as much as possible—from the capital city to the Great Lakes region, the vast corn and wheat belts and cattle country, the Rocky Mountains, and the scenic western coast line.

To allow for the participation of as many people as possible in a conference that was to write a plan affecting all the peoples of the world, a host of consultants and advisers was invited to assist each delegation, and while the delegates themselves would make the final decisions they had the benefit of specialized advice from every level of interest. Forty-two organizations were invited to send consultants to the American delegation. Labor, agriculture, industry, educational and religious groups were represented.

Before the list was even shown to her, Mrs. Roosevelt's terse comment was, "We must have Mrs. Bethune."

Others phoned or wrote, asking to be assured that Mrs. Bethune would attend the San Francisco Conference.

As a matter of fact, she was not on the list, and the National Council of Negro Women was not one of the forty-two, since it was still fairly new. Not daring to reopen the list lest a flood of requests come in from other groups clamoring to be represented, and realizing that the list would defeat its own purpose if it were extended indefinitely, the committee on arrangements looked over its records. The National Association for the Advancement of Colored People had been invited to send one consultant and two alternates, and so far it had indicated only two names, Walter White as delegate and William E. Burghardt DuBois as alternate. A phone call to Walter White explaining the predicament was all that was needed, and he assured them that the N.A.A.C.P. would be glad to choose Mrs. Bethune as its second alternate. Since she was an officer in both organizations she could, in effect, represent both.

Mrs. Bethune was still very much driven by her responsibilities in the war effort and hampered by her asthma. After hearing of her appointment to the San Francisco Conference and obtaining permission to have Dr. Ferebee make the trip with her so that her asthma attacks would not impede her work, she hurried to Texas to speak at Wiley and Bishop College in Marshall, Sam Huston College in Austin, and a mass meeting in Dallas. Dr. James Lowell Hall, an asthma specialist, at that time Superintendent of Freedmen's Hospital in Washington, D.C., accompanied her to Texas, sitting in the audience whenever she spoke, so that he could signal her to stop speaking at the end of twenty minutes. He knew the limits of her strength far better than she did.

She stayed at the home of a friend in Dallas, and while they sat in the living room chatting one evening, Dr. Hall rushed in and interrupted them, grief and shock in his face.

"I don't want you to excite yourself," he said. "But I have very bad news for you, the worst possible news."

"Tell us quickly."

"President Roosevelt is dead. The news has just come over the radio."

Mrs. Bethune sat stunned and silent, trying to understand what she had just heard, trying to realize that the great personality who was only sixty-three years old, the friend of the underprivileged, was gone.

The President had been in his cottage at Warm Springs,

Georgia, chatting with his physician in front of the fireplace
while an artist made sketches, when he looked up and said,
"I have a terrific headache."

Within a few minutes he lost consciousness and had to be
carried to his bed. He died that same afternoon, just before
the final military victories in Europe and the Pacific and before the nations of the world came together in San Francisco
for the meetings that he had been so instrumental in bringing
about.

When Mrs. Bethune was able to collect herself, she sent an
eloquent telegram to Mrs. Roosevelt and boarded a plane for
Washington, discovering at the end of the dreary flight that
the President's body would be brought to Washington the
next day and that she was to appear on a nationwide memorial radio program to speak for minority groups.

The funeral services were held in the East Room of the
White House. On one side Mrs. Roosevelt and her family sat
in the gold-brocaded chairs of honor, the new President,
Harry S. Truman, and his family, Foreign Minister Anthony
Eden and other diplomats, representatives and delegations,
and among them Mary McLeod Bethune.

"I looked at the flag-draped bier and my mind went back
to the time when we first met and I had moved him to tears
by my impassioned plea for my people's rights. I recalled
holding his hands and looking into his fine, strong face, and
telling him how much the common people depended on him.
I remembered all this and many other wonderful little things
that he had done for me and for my people."

One episode after another flashed through her memory—
of the many times she had chatted with him, put completely
at ease by his charm. There was one humorous situation when
she, Channing Tobias, and Walter White were called in to
discuss the problem of redistribution centers for Negro soldiers. Suddenly the President lighted a cigarette and passed

the pack to Mrs. Bethune, who shook her head in the negative.

"Well, now," the President teased her. "When are you go-ing to learn how to smoke?"

Her gay reply was, "I will smoke with you in celebration of your re-election this coming fall."

The way he nodded and said, "All right, that is good," plainly showed his deep affection for her.

Now she sat in the East Room, gazing at his bier, and wept uncontrolledly, like everyone else around her and around the world. How would the Conference fare without his guid-ing genius? It had been one of his great dreams, and he would not be there to see it open.

Still grief-stricken, the eyes of the world turned upon Cal-ifornia less than two weeks later, on April 25, 1945, to watch with hope and prayer as four hundred delegates and some fifteen hundred consultants, secretaries, bodyguards, re-porters, and observers gathered in the San Francisco Opera House. The great stage was decorated with columns of the flags of the nations, and in the audience sat people of every dress: saris, turbans, fezzes, tailored continental suits, home-spun; their skins black, brown, golden, and white. White faces were conspicuously in the minority when the whole world was brought together.

The San Francisco Conference was convened to write the charter for the United Nations Organization, gathering to-gether the findings and ideas of all previous conferences, and especially the Dumbarton Oaks proposals, plus the suggestions that the delegates brought from their own countries, where their legislatures had debated each item.

The delegates divided into committees so that each could work on a special section of the Charter—the Preamble, the Security Council, the General Assembly, the Trusteeship Council, and so on—and came together in plenary session to put the results together.

When Mary McLeod Bethune went to San Francisco, she was taking her rightful place among the outstanding personalities of the world. She was especially interested in the sections working on human rights and on the trusteeships to be established over colonies that had been formerly owned by the Axis powers. Her great value lay, not in any profound or extensive knowledge, but in her expertness in getting on with people. She was a speaker who always had her audience with her, a suave diplomat, a prodigious writer of letters, who was actually meeting with a host of friends when she went to San Francisco. Her contacts had already been made with the Far Eastern and Middle Eastern peoples; her files were full of letters from Burma, India, Syria, Indonesia, the Philippines, Ceylon, the Caribbean.

"This is something that must advance the welfare of the people who live at the very bottom of the economic level," she was heard to say often. "I am speaking for people of all races and all creeds who expect the new world to mean this for them."

The conference had plenty of lawyers and other specialists; Mrs. Bethune was interested in human beings and their aspirations; she was an interpreter of popular emotion, a spokesman for the underdog; and while she did not speak often, and then only briefly, in the meetings to which she was invited, she always had a specific contribution to offer.

Each afternoon during the two months of the Conference there was a large forum, some two hundred observers, and Mrs. Bethune frequently addressed this group, speaking with her usual clarity and courage.

Mr. White, Dr. DuBois, and Mrs. Bethune went to the West Coast with high hopes for a World Bill of Rights, and since they were in the best possible position to speak for the minorities of the world, they planned their approach carefully. Walter White issued their official statement:

"It is our hope as consultants to the American delegation to induce the San Francisco Conference to face what is one of the most serious problems of the twentieth century—the question of race and color. We are particularly concerned with what is done about colonial empires and the well-being of colonial peoples around the world. Most of these colonial peoples are colored. What happens to even the most exploited of these has direct bearing upon the future of Negroes in the United States."

Their influence was both felt and respected. They sat in conference after conference, helping to write, rewrite, and revise each sentence and paragraph of the Charter. They met with the press and with Negro groups that came to the city to be in closer touch with those who were working on the inside.

All of the specialized consultants did the same. As a matter of fact, the consultants did a better reporting job than the press, because they were closer to what was really going on and could send mimeographed reports back to the groups they represented. The consultants were in on the most urgent secrets of state, and never once did one of them betray a confidence.

At last the finished Charter was published in five languages: Chinese, English, Russian, French, and Spanish; and the last big session met in the Opera House so that the delegates could sign the document and reaffirm their hopes that all the governments of the world would some day accept the Charter of the United Nations as international law.

The United Nations had three great purposes:

To remove the causes of war by creating friendly relations among peoples and establishing fundamental human rights everywhere.

To provide means for adjusting dangerous differences between nations.

To build collective security against acts of aggression and other threats to peace.

It was the hope of the enslaved peoples of the world.

"Something that must advance the welfare of the people who live at the very bottom," Mrs. Bethune had said.

She did not remain for the final session. When she had done as much as she could, she left one of her alternates in her seat and returned East.

Tired and ill, she leaned heavily on Dr. Ferebee's arm as they mounted the steps of the Council House on Vermont Avenue. Her face was lighted by a smile and her eyes glistened with happiness as a result of all she had done and witnessed. She knew the trend of the times was at last toward racial equality. Soon there would be an end to separate entrances and knocking on back doors. Three years later her optimism was still further vindicated when the United Nations General Assembly issued its Universal Declaration of Human Rights.

The seventy-year-old consultant on international problems sank into a chair before her desk on the second floor. Yes, she was tired, she admitted, as she rested her snow-white head in her hands for a moment.

There waiting for her was a long slim package.

"Open it for me," she said to her secretary.

The wrappings were torn away to reveal a heavy oak walking stick, its highly polished shaft delicately carved to resemble gnarled wood, at its top a silver plate bearing the name of the late Franklin Delano Roosevelt. Attached to it was an affectionate note from the President's widow, who wanted her to accept it in remembrance of their association.

Mary Bethune took the cane in her hands and ran her fingertips along its surface. Symbol of love and strength, she would carry it with her always.

May hills lean toward you
Hills and windswept mountains
And trees be happy
That have seen you pass.

"Benediction" by Donald Jeffrey Hayes

20. *Today in a White Man's World*

I am at my zenith now," Mary Mc-
Leod Bethune wrote in 1946 from her desk at the Council
House in Washington. "You would think I was an executive
getting $50,000! From the Atlantic and the Pacific come calls
to this desk. They call me from the government departments,
the War Department, the Navy, as if I were a paid person.
People just come to me."

They came highborn and low, young and old, just as her
family crowded around her for their first letters when she
brought home her brand-new knowledge from Miss Wilson's
school, as her own students clung to her for protection during
a Klan demonstration, as her college staff sat in conference
with her, trying to match her courage and vision.

The wisdom that others sought to share created a college whose property is valued at over a million dollars and which accommodates nearly nine hundred undergraduate and adult students in its day and evening schools. It has been a full four-year college only since 1946, and it has already received an "A" rating from the State Department of Education and from the Southern Association of Colleges and Secondary Schools.

Her personality still dominates the campus, even though she is no longer there to be active in school administration. Each Freshman class makes a pilgrimage to the original Oak Street site, to remind the younger generation of the hardships and sacrifices that went into the creation of the school they might otherwise take for granted. When new teachers bring to the college ideas conflicting with what she advocated—they may want to allow the students to smoke on the campus, or they may want to see the school switch from its emphasis on industrial training to a purely academic program—they find themselves confronted by a forceful opposition. Sometimes they remain and adjust; sometimes they go on to the staff of another college.

Money continues to be the biggest worry, and fund raising is an ever-present chore. B-C needs an endowment fund that will provide it with sufficient income to meet its operating costs.

The money specter haunts most Negro colleges, and the smaller ones operate on desperately small budgets. Taking the whole situation into consideration in 1943, President F. D. Patterson of Tuskegee Institute hit upon the idea of a co-operative fund-raising plan for all Negro colleges, so that the smallest and least known would benefit from the reputation and popularity of the larger ones. After publishing his idea for a combined effort in the Pittsburgh *Courier*, he met with college presidents, directors of foundations, educators and philanthropists, and the result was the United Negro College Fund which each year conducts one large fund-raising campaign that reaches hundreds of new donors and is able to distribute funds to thirty-two colleges and universities. Mrs. Bethune threw herself passionately into the work to establish the United Negro College Fund, and Bethune-Cookman is one of the colleges that benefit from it.

Mrs. Bethune watched the parade of history pass by from Reconstruction days. She saw the American Negro make startling and heroic progress in the face of every disadvantage, emerging as an individual of culture, dignity, and talent. Other Negro leaders of today hope that another fifty years will bring him a greater participation in his own government, equal opportunity to enter the best universities, professions, and trades, and complete disappearance of segregation in work, school, church, and community.

"Today in a white man's world I cannot eat in a hotel," she wrote during her N.Y.A. days. "But I have the satisfaction of knowing that my skin is as clean as that of anyone in the hotel, that I have a shining white bathroom, that my home is spotless; and my soul is beyond such pettiness. The other day in New York City I went to keep an appointment and the elevator boy refused to carry me up to the office. He told me to use the freight elevator. I refused. 'You lump all Negroes together, don't you?' I said to him. 'They're all maids to you, I suppose. What would you think if I told you all white people were elevator boys?' The young man permitted me to ride up with him."

Two decades have passed since that episode. In the same white man's world she, as an individual, completely broke through the barriers of race, and her associates of every description found it difficult to remember what color Mrs. Bethune was.

The touch of her hand will be forever on the community

of Daytona, where she reclaimed both land and souls. West of B-C campus, rows of attractive, low-priced houses have replaced the unhealthy shanties of a few years ago. This is Pinehaven, another of Mrs. Bethune's achievements. In the 1930's, when the Works Progress Administration was distributing funds for slum-clearance programs, she thought immediately of Colored Town, conferred with housing officials in other cities, then hurried back to Daytona to call a huge mass meeting. Everyone wanted a slum-clearance project, but no one knew what to do about it until "Mother" Bethune directed them to form a housing authority, select an executive secretary, and make application to the government for funds.

The local real-estate agents raised a hue and cry, claiming that the project would compete with their business; but the combined influence of Mrs. Bethune and Mrs. Roosevelt turned the trick. In 1938 the first low-rent units were completed, admitting only tenants whose income was less than $3000 a year and charging $10 to $37 monthly rent. In a few months the units were filled with families who had never before in their lives enjoyed electric lights or flush toilets. Sixty-six more units went up a year later, and there are others under construction.

That accomplished, Mrs. Bethune turned her attention to the fact that Negroes of Daytona did not have any beach. Some Negro children grew up without ever having seen the ocean. Approaching two or three of her influential and sympathetic white friends, she persuaded them to acquire two and a half miles of ocean front, which is now being developed as a resort section for Negroes, with summer cottages, bathing pavilions, and hotels—the Volusia Beach Project.

This grand old lady at seventy started every day with a prayer, and she still depended for encouragement upon "The

Optimist's Good Morning," the slim volume full of wisdom presented to her so many years ago by John D. Rockefeller. She could walk briskly up long flights of stairs, work night and day, and exhaust anyone who tried to collaborate with her.

Ruth Brall, the sculptor, discovered this to her dismay when she established herself in the Council House to make a head of Mary McLeod Bethune. Petite, vivacious, golden-blond, and talented, she lost ten pounds during her short visit and at last had to say, "Please, Mrs. Bethune. I can work all day, or all night; I can't do both."

After a full day, Mrs. Bethune would keep her talking far into the night, and be amazed when she didn't appear for an early breakfast.

During the day Mrs. Bethune would pose for a short period, dash off to answer some mail, give instructions, or consult with a high-ranking official, whisk through the room again, while the artist pleaded, "Can you hold that pose for a second? Please, that expression; I almost got it."

Mrs. Brall worked on in the midst of bedlam, almost entirely without rest, watching the world beat a path to the Council House door. She caught intimate glimpses of Mrs. Bethune's rare, many-sided personality, her quick-changing moods. She watched her smuggle in gingerbread and eat it in spite of Dr. Ferebee's orders to the contrary. Mrs. Bethune loves gingerbread and will go to almost any lengths to get it, even though the violation of diet may bring on an asthma attack. Reaching down into her desk drawer she would bring out a piece of the precious stuff and eat it like a naughty child, saying to Mrs. Brall:

"You won't tell on me, will you?"

"No; I won't tell."

During one sitting she was overtaken by such a severe attack that she had to be carried to bed, seemingly breathing her last. When Dr. Ferebee wanted to know what she had eaten, she answered slyly:

"Ask the girl who brought up my tray. She knows what she gave me."

Ruth Brall was amply repaid for all the anguish and exhaustion when Mrs. Bethune looked at the finished portrait and nodded her complete approval. The artist had seen her as she really was and had interpreted her accurately. As she turned the head slowly around and watched its expression change, Mrs. Bethune paid the sculptor warm compliments on the results of her talent.

The Bethune portrait was one of a series that Mrs. Brall has done of contemporary Negro leaders. She is a widely recognized artist, having received awards from Allied Artists of America, Painters and Sculptors Society of New Jersey, and the Pen and Brush Society, and having given as many as three one-man shows in a year. In 1949 she set aside all of her other work to devote herself to her twelve Negro portraits: Mrs. Bethune, Dr. Bunche, Mr. White, Dr. DuBois, Dr. Tobias, Mr. Randolph, Jackie Robinson, and others. The completed series was exhibited for the benefit of the United Negro College Fund in stores, libraries, and colleges.

The Bethune assignment, she felt, was the most amazing experience of all, and none afforded her quite such a wealth of episodes and anecdotes.

One day during a sitting, Mrs. Bethune rested her elbows on a pile of correspondence, cupped her palms together, and prayed suddenly: "Dear Lord, send me a hundred men and a hundred women with a hundred dollars each." She was up to her old game of fund raising.

About an hour later, a distinguished member of the State Department walked in and embraced her affectionately. She gazed up at him coyly and said, "That, Sir, will cost you one hundred dollars."

His visit proved to be expensive, because he was not allowed to leave until he had delivered up the sum.

"You see, Mrs. Brall? My prayer was answered," she boasted triumphantly.

"Could it be your sex appeal?"

"I? At my age? Why, I have four great-grandchildren."

The sculptor was amazed at Mrs. Bethune's marvelous self-control, too, when she had to talk over the telephone to a member of the white social set. Her cast-iron calm, her tightened face muscles, her steady tone of voice indicated rudeness at the other end of the wire. Mrs. Bethune was asking permission for the use of a hall.

"How could you take that from that woman?" Mrs. Brall demanded. "Why didn't you tell her off?"

"That is just what she was waiting for me to do. If I had become angry I wouldn't have gotten the hall."

The indomitable Mrs. Bethune never remained at the Council House for long at a time: too many commitments in one state or another. The State Teachers Association invited her to address one of its meetings in Columbia, South Carolina, at the city Auditorium; and South Carolina's favorite and most outstanding daughter drew hundreds besides the Association members, who applauded their palms red for Mary Jane McLeod. With her on the platform were prominent leaders of both races, among them a slim, white-haired lady who came forward when Mrs. Bethune had finished speaking and threw her arms around her and kissed her. She was Miss Essie Wilson, daughter of the man who had owned Mrs. Bethune's mother. Miss Wilson had been in China as a missionary and had just returned to discover the heights to which the pigtailed cottonpicker had risen.

In February 1949, Mrs. Bethune went to Winter Park, Florida, to receive the honorary degree of Doctor of Humanities from Rollins College, having already been granted honorary degrees by nine other colleges.

"Please rest a little; be more cautious," her doctors pleaded, knowing full well they were talking to the west wind, because she had just been invited to spend ten days in Haiti as a guest of the government.

Haiti, the "Black Republic," occupies the western half of the island of Hispaniola in the Caribbean Sea just east of Cuba. A self-governing, independent country with a largely Negro population, its lush tropical valleys and mountains were once filled with bloodshed and revolution. It was a French possession until the slaves themselves rose up in insurrection and drove out their white rulers. Since then the progress of the country has been an inspiration to colored peoples everywhere.

"Queen Mary" Bethune stepped from a Pan-American clipper at Port-au-Prince, the Haitian capital, on July 12, 1949, to plunge into a schedule of conferences, tours, receptions, dinners, and homage. President and Mme. Dumarsais Estime held a full-dress reception for her at the National Palace; the Minister of Foreign Affairs did the same; the American Embassy gave a luncheon. She went into the rural areas on an escorted tour of schools, farms, orphanages, and baby clinics, and the crowning event of her visit was receiving Haiti's highest award, the gold Medal of Honor and Merit, with its blue center and white enameled cross.

When she left, the streets were lined with admirers, waving their hands and cheering as her car passed, calling after her, "Live long! Live long! Come back! Come back!"

"Haiti and I fell in love with each other," she wrote in *Women United*, the official magazine of the National Council. "I returned to America with two cherished possessions presented to me by the Government of Haiti: the Order of Honor and Merit, Haiti's highest decoration, given to a woman for the first time in its history; and a lovely wood carving of a peasant woman, the woman I met striding along the mountain roads every day of my visit."

In the autumn she stepped down as president of the National Council of Negro Women, handing the gavel she herself had created and held for so many years to Dr. Dorothy Boulding Ferebee, in a gathering of brilliant, first-magnitude personalities. The fourteenth annual convention of the National Council—its theme, "World Citizenship through Human Understanding"—lasted for three days in November 1949, and ended in a gala meeting in the auditorium of the Labor Department in Washington. Mrs. Bethune called it "International Night" to commemorate the fourth anniversary of the founding of the United Nations.

The entire two front rows were filled with members of various embassies. President Harry S. Truman, whose schedule usually allows him to make only a late arrival and an early departure, arrived at eight-thirty and remained through the entire affair. On the speakers' platform with Mrs. Bethune and the President were Dr. Ralph Bunche, Maurice J. Tobin, Secretary of Labor, Aubrey Williams, and other notables.

Dressed in a long black velvet gown, her snow-white hair glistening under the intense television lights, the Haitian cross suspended around her neck, white gardenias on her shoulder, her program broadcast to the world over the "Voice of America," Mary McLeod Bethune had truly reached her zenith on this night as she presided.

Her theme when she addressed the audience was the Universal Declaration of Human Rights evolved by the United

Nations. "Let us not be too impatient at the seemingly slow progress we are now making toward the goal of world peace," she cautioned her illustrious listeners.

She nodded happily when Secretary of Labor Tobin reported that ten states now have laws banning discriminatory practices in the labor field, and when Mme. Pandit asked the women of India and the United States to join hands in the promotion of world peace.

President Truman's message was more personal. "I join with your members in thanking you for your leadership, which will forever be an inspiration to those who seek to carry forward the noble purposes to which your life has been devoted."

The cameras flashed and clicked all during the program, and the news reporters crowded around the platform to take picture after picture of Mrs. Bethune as she stood beaming with joy and gratitude, flanked on one side by the President of the United States and on the other by the Ambassador from India. When the program came to an end, the great assemblage rose to its feet to applaud.

Their autographed pictures line the walls of her study in Daytona, this vast gallery of great men and women who have been her devoted friends. A visitor may gaze in amazement at the collection of more than a hundred and thirty photographs of international celebrities, in the place of honor a large reproduction of the Salisbury portrait of the late President Roosevelt. There are gifts and curios from all over the world—tapestries from India, a pair of hand-carved ebony elephants from Africa.

On her seventy-fifth birthday, telegrams and letters of congratulations flooded in from publishers, legislators, Supreme Court justices, churchmen, scientists, labor leaders, businessmen, humble field hands—all begging to be counted. Mrs.

Pandit sent the orchid she wanted her to wear, together with a magnificent basket of flowers.

The following year she was elected president of the Central Life Insurance Company in Tampa.

She sat in the councils of the great, and she was mother to the lowly, for she never lost her touch with the common people. When she returned to Mayesville, South Carolina, for a visit in 1950, she was as much at home in the share-cropper cabins as she was in the White House.

She walked along the dirt road she had covered so often on her way to school and looked across the fields where she had once picked two hundred fifty pounds of cotton a day. The McLeod cabin was gone, and the only monument that marked its place was a solitary fig tree. She made a pilgrimage to the school that Miss Wilson had created and found it in a woeful state of disrepair. After more than sixty years, it was still the only school open to the Negro children of Mayesville.

She shook her aged head. There was so much yet to be done! Unequal educational opportunities, inadequate housing, poverty!

The white mansions of the erstwhile slave owners were gone; their whole era had passed. How she had once been awed by the huge, two-story-high pillars of the old Wilson estate! When she remembered the childhood episode in the playhouse of the Wilson grandchildren, she knew that deep down in her secret heart there remained a lingering prayer: that the day may come when no child anywhere in the world will have to flinch under the stinging words,

"Put down that book. *You* can't read!"

Epilogue

Mrs. Bethune's last five years were spent in an increasing retirement at her home in Daytona Beach, Florida, until, on May 18, 1955, a heart attack brought her life to a close. Her passing marked the end of a fruitful career, one that had enriched countless other lives and had advanced the cause of racial equality all over the United States. She was one of the very early pioneers in this field, a contemporary of Booker T. Washington, and she lived long enough to see the building well advanced upon the foundations she had helped to lay. In her later years she watched with deep satisfaction as Negro Americans moved into more and more new areas of employment, into equality in the armed forces, and into integrated church memberships; and just a year before her death the Supreme Court of the United States rendered its decision that segregated schools are unconstitutional. That must have been thrilling news indeed for the woman who had once founded a school for Negro children on a public dump heap with a total capital of a dollar and fifty cents.

Selected Bibliography

BOOKS

ARNE, SIGRID. *United Nations Primer*. New York: Rinehart & Company, Inc., 1945

BARTLETT, ROBERT M. *They Did Something About It*. New York: Association Press, 1939

BROWN, INA CORINNE. *Race Relations in a Democracy*. New York: Harper & Bros., 1949

CHAPMAN, REV. J. WILBUR. *The Life and Work of Dwight L. Moody*. Chicago: John C. Winston Co., 1900

DANIEL, SADIE IOLA. *Women Builders*. Washington, D.C.: The Associated Publishers, Inc., 1931

DANIELS, REV. WILLIAM HAVEN. *D. L. Moody and His Work*. Hartford: American Publishing Co., 1876

DAVIE, MAURICE R. *Negroes in American Society*. New York: Whittlesey House, 1949

DUBOIS, WILLIAM EDWARD BURGHARDT. *The Gift of Black Folk*. Boston: The Stratford Co., 1924

EMBREE, EDWIN R. *Thirteen Against the Odds*. New York: The Viking Press, 1944

FINKELSTEIN, LOUIS (editor). *American Spiritual Autobiographies; Fifteen Self-Portraits*. New York: Harper & Bros., 1948

FRANKLIN, JOHN HOPE. *From Slavery to Freedom*. New York: Alfred A. Knopf, 1948

GALT, TOM. *How the United Nations Works*. New York: Thomas Y. Crowell Company, 1947

HOLT, RACKHAM. *George Washington Carver, an American Biography*. Garden City, N.Y.: Doubleday, Doran and Company, 1943

HUGHES, LANGSTON, AND BONTEMPS, ARNA (editors). *The Poetry of the Negro, 1746–1949*. Garden City, N.Y.: Doubleday & Company, Inc., 1949

KONVITZ, MILTON R. *The Constitution and Civil Rights*. New York: Columbia University Press, 1947

LINDLEY, BETTY AND ERNEST K. *A New Deal for Youth*. New York: The Viking Press, 1938

LOGAN, RAYFORD W. (editor). *What the Negro Wants*. Chapel Hill: The University of North Carolina Press, 1944

LORWIN, LEWIS L. *Youth Work Programs, Problems and Policies*. Washington, D.C.: American Council on Education, 1941

MANGUM, CHARLES S., JR. *The Legal Status of the Negro*. Chapel Hill: The University of North Carolina Press, 1940

MARSHALL, HARRIET GIBBS. *The Story of Haiti*. Boston: The Christopher Publishing House, 1930

MOTON, ROBERT RUSSA. *What the Negro Thinks*. Garden City, N.Y.: Garden City Publishing Company, 1942

OTTLEY, ROI. *New World A-Coming*. Cleveland: The World Publishing Company, 1943

RICHARDSON, BEN. *Great American Negroes*. New York: Thomas Y. Crowell Company, 1945

ROSE, ARNOLD M. *The Negro's Morale*. Minneapolis: The University of Minnesota Press, 1949

SCOTT, EMMETT J., AND STOWE, LYMAN BEECHER. *Booker T. Washington, Builder of a Civilization*. Garden City, N.Y.: Doubleday, Page & Company, 1916

SIMKINS, FRANCIS BUTLER. *South Carolina During Reconstruction*. Chapel Hill: The University of North Carolina Press, 1932

SMITH, LILLIAN. *Killers of the Dream*. New York: W. W. Norton & Company, 1949

STOCKBRIDGE, FRANK PARKER, AND PERRY, JOHN HOLLIDAY. *So This Is Florida*. Jacksonville: John H. Perry Publishing Co., 1938

VANCE, RUPERT B. *Human Factors in Cotton Culture*. Chapel Hill: The University of North Carolina Press, 1929

WASHINGTON, BOOKER T. *Up from Slavery, an Autobiography*. New York: The Sun Dial Press, Inc., 1937

WHITE, WALTER. *A Man Called White*. New York: The Viking Press, 1948

WILSON, RUTH DANENHOWER. *Jim Crow Joins Up*. New York: Press of William J. Clark, 1944

WINSLOW, THACHER, AND DAVIDSON, FRANK P. *American Youth, an Enforced Reconnaissance*. Cambridge, Mass.: Harvard University Press, 1940

MAGAZINE ARTICLES

BETHUNE, MARY MCLEOD. "The Problems of the City Dweller." *Opportunity*, February, 1925

———. "I'll Never Turn Back No More!" *Opportunity*, November, 1938

———. "Faith That Moved a Dump Heap." *Who*, June, 1941

———. "Our Stake in Tomorrow's World." *Aframerican Woman's Journal*, June, 1945

———. "My Secret Talks with F.D.R." *Ebony*, April, 1949

———. "Haiti Was Wonderful." *Women United*, October, 1949

———. "True Leadership Is Timeless." *Negro History Bulletin*, May, 1950

"Bethune-Cookman Collegiate Institute." *Southwestern Christian Advocate*, January 20, 1927

BOOBYER, HARRIET S. "Mary McLeod Bethune." *Womens Missionary Magazine of the United Presbyterian Church*, October, 1936

BROWN, WILLIAM GARROTT. "The Ku Klux Klan Movement." *Atlantic Monthly*, June, 1901

BYRON, DORA. "From 'A Cabin in the Cotton'" *Opportunity*, April, 1936

CANSLER, MILDRED A. "Mary McLeod Bethune." *Women's Missionary Magazine of the United Presbyterian Church*, August, 1930

CHAMBERLAIN, DANIEL H. "Reconstruction in South Carolina." *Atlantic Monthly*, April, 1901

EDWARDES, CHARLES. "A Scene from Florida Life." *Living Age*, September 13, 1884

HERRICK, GENEVIEVE FORBES. "Loved, Feared and Followed." *Collier's*, September 23, 1950

"The Life of Mary McLeod Bethune." *Our World*, December, 1950

"Matriarch." *Time*, July 22, 1946

McGUIRE, ROBERTA. "Negro Angel." *Aframerican Woman's Journal*, September, 1945

OTTLEY, ROI. "The Big Ten Who Run Negro America." *Negro Digest*, May, 1948

SIMKINS, FRANCIS B. "The Ku Klux Klan in South Carolina, 1868–1871." *Journal of Negro History*, July, 1927

"Singer and Citizen." *Newsweek*, April 25, 1949

THURMAN, SUE BAILEY. "Behind the Scenes at San Francisco." *Aframerican Woman's Journal*, June, 1945

TORREY, BRADFORD. "On the St. Augustine Road." *Atlantic Monthly*, September, 1893

———. "On the Beach at Daytona." *Atlantic Monthly*, July, 1894

TRENT, W. J., JR. "An Adventure in Cooperation." *Journal of Educational Sociology*, April, 1946

WILLIAMS, DAN. "The Cotton Picker Still Sings." *Washington Post*, May, 1946

WILSON, RUTH DANENHOWER. "Negro Colleges of Liberal Arts." *American Scholar*, Autumn, 1950